Is Your Boss Making You Sick?

IS YOUR BOSS MAKING YOU SICK?

THE **8** E'S OF EQUILIBRIUM
TO MASTER
WORK-LIFE BALANCE

DAVID LEE

NEW YORK

LONDON • NASHVILLE • MELBOURNE • VANCOUVER

Is Your Boss Making You Sick?

The 8 E's of Equilibrium to Master Work-Life Balance

Published in New York, New York, by Morgan James Publishing. Morgan James is a trademark of Morgan James, LLC. www.MorganJamesPublishing.com

Proudly distributed by Publishers Group West®

A **FREE** ebook edition is available for you or a friend with the purchase of this print book.

CLEARLY SIGN YOUR NAME ABOVE

Instructions to claim your free ebook edition:
1. Visit MorganJamesBOGO.com
2. Sign your name CLEARLY in the space above
3. Complete the form and submit a photo of this entire page
4. You or your friend can download the ebook to your preferred device

ISBN 9781636982809 paperback
ISBN 9781636982816 ebook
Library of Congress Control Number:
2023943305

Cover and Interior Design by:
Chris Treccani
www.3dogcreative.net

Morgan James is a proud partner of Habitat for Humanity Peninsula and Greater Williamsburg. Partners in building since 2006.

Get involved today! Visit: www.morgan-james-publishing.com/giving-back

Disclaimer

To order additional books:

www.amazon.com

www.mindandbodymastery.com.au

Printed in the USA

To my father, Matthew Edward Lee, the scariest man of my youth
and the fondest man of my adulthood, who instilled in me
the dream of lifelong learning.

"Do the simple things well, and everything else will take care of itself."

—Matt Lee, 1936–2021

TABLE OF CONTENTS

FOREWORD

I neither needed nor sought a life coach.

I had just hoped for a personal trainer to help me get fit and healthy again after having a family. I did not recognize the degree to which I could benefit from David Lee's advice. I did not realize the importance of focusing not only on a healthy body, but on a healthy strategy for having a satisfying and fulfilling "dash" on my tombstone. To allow me to truly appreciate my bit of time on Earth, my time with my family and friends.

Somewhere between getting back into the gym and climbing back onto the bike, I began to recognize that I had gears I had never used before. Now I can plank for eight minutes—one minute for each of the recommended 8 E's—the "Leeway" to achieving and now maintaining my equilibrium. Now, not only am I physically fit and healthy again, but my life has more direction, and I have a method for ensuring a balanced strategy for an ongoing sense of fulfilment. I had not previously recognized the importance of this.

Contained in the pages of this book are the stories that caught and captivated me, the strategies that focused and then guided me, and the tools that provided me with the opportunity to find happiness, fulfilment, and yes, the equilibrium for my future.

This book reflects the manner in which David provides his coaching, and I have seen many of David's clients benefit from his quick-witted wisdom, experience, and kindness. He has a rare ability to immediately reframe and navigate whatever the current obstacle or inappropriate paradigm is. For me, any hurdle, setback, or challenge that I outlined to David was met with an on-point, redefining question, and then the epiphany would invariably follow the laughter.

The 8 E's of Equilibrium provide entertainment, but they also provide a framework for navigating a healthy and fulfilling life. Prevention is better than cure. So much better. This is as true in medicine as it is in ensuring one can truly experience life's vitality. The old nursery rhyme sums it up best: "The best six doctors anywhere, and no one can deny it, are sunshine, water, air and rest, exercise, and diet."

I have been working as a doctor for over 15 years. I find what I do so very rewarding and am so very grateful for the privilege of helping people when they need it. And yet, some of the treatment that medicine provides is stuck on trying to correct the errors of an unhealthy life with pills and quick fixes when the reality is that some of these ailments can be avoided.

I sincerely suggest you read and apply the wisdom contained in the following pages and avoid coming to see me in the emergency department. And you might—you just might—find the secret to your happiness. So, where life does give you a choice, choose you.

Dr. Celia Bentley
Emergency Physician, BSc (Psych), MBBS, FACEM

INTRODUCTION

"It's not at all that we have too short a time to live, but that we squander a great deal of it. Life is long enough, and it's given in sufficient measure to do many great things if we spend it well. And so it is. We don't receive a short life, we make it so."
—Seneca

W hen I first started my coaching career, I was contracted to consult with an organization in the areas of increased productivity and time management.

Arriving at their offices, I was greeted by a bubbly young coordinator, who told me enthusiastically that this was her first full-time job. She politely offered me a coffee and made me feel at home. I was impressed.

The CEO told me he was proud of his new coordinator. She was a real go-getter, someone he had great hopes for in his business and the industry at large.

Less than three years later, I received a phone call from the same CEO asking to meet again. Once again, I was met by the same young coordinator who greeted me on my first visit to their office—but she was not the same person at all.

She was at least 20 kilos (44 pounds) heavier and lacked *any* of the vim and vigor she displayed when I first met her. She offered me a coffee, but this time she placed it out of my reach on a coaster on the boardroom table and turned away without a word. I called after her to say thanks and received a half-hearted smile, probably because I had remembered her name.

The CEO briefed me on the newest assignment, which involved the launch of a new product line. As our meeting wrapped up, I asked him about the coordinator, and he told me that she was now his personal assistant—but he had not noticed her change in temperament.

A few weeks later at the product launch cocktail party, feeling everything was going so well, I approached the personal assistant, to check that she was happy with how the event was going. Her opinion seemed negative and so I asked her how she felt in herself, commenting she seemed a bit different from when I had first met her.

I am fortunate that whenever I ask people how they are, they never beat around the bush with their answers and tell me the whole truth and nothing but the truth. People I have just met will often reveal their darkest secrets, and then tell me they have no idea why they told me.

She was miserable and pessimistic. The job was robbing her of a social life and any of life's other pleasures. I asked her what she did for exercise because I'm a firm believer that a healthy body wills a healthy mind.

She did not have time for exercise, she said. Her monotonous morning routine went like this: rise at 7am, shower, drive to the train station, catch up on sleep on the train, arrive at the office 90 minutes later.

She still lived with her parents.

Her evenings were no less boring and repetitive. She regularly went to bed at midnight after spending most of the night watching television with her parents. She was almost literally killing time, and it was having a terrible effect on her self-esteem.

When I asked her to score her physical and mental health out of 10, all she could muster was a 3 for both. She was tired all the time, regularly caught colds, and had not visited the doctor in over two years, lamenting that at one stage she was very fit. A familiar story I often hear.

I felt sorry for her, but I could see that even a small change would benefit her. I asked if I could send her some ideas for wellness and if she would consider going to bed an hour earlier and rising an hour earlier, so that she could use the extra morning time to put them into effect, all designed to stimulate her body and mind. She said that she would try.

Many years later, post-COVID lockdown, I was contacted by another organization to workshop strategies for their return to the office. I had created a program during the pandemic centered on resilience, overcoming adversity, and work-life balance, and this was my first in-person workshop in two years.

I gain composure before any presentation with breathing techniques and remind myself of all the research and preparation I have done. The advice I give to anxious presenters is always the same: look for a friendly face in the audience for reassurance, and look to them whenever you feel nervous, remembering that nobody wants to see you fail.

I didn't have to look far. Beaming up at me from the front row was the same young woman I had met on my very first coaching assignment. I say "the same," as I could see she was now at least 20 kilos (44 pounds) leaner than when I had last seen her.

Her youthful enthusiasm had returned too. In the first break of the workshop, she jumped out of her seat and hugged me, telling me she was now a sales director and was incredibly grateful for the conversation we had all those years ago at the cocktail party.

She had taken a few weeks to open my email, but on a "down day," as she called it, while working from her bed at home, she took my advice and decided to take the first step. She downloaded the template I'd attached and followed the steps of my program. She ditched the mindless hours of television and joined a gym, where she met her partner. Together they had bought a house and produced two beautiful daughters.

We chatted for a while and what impressed me most was her perspective on the preciousness of time and her attitude toward a harmonious work-life balance.

On my drive home, I felt a real sense of joy for this young woman. It's the same joy I feel after having helped teams and individuals achieve life-changing breakthroughs—whether that be in the boardroom, café, or beside a hardworking client on a treadmill in a private training session.

This book is designed for the time-poor individual who feels disconnected from time itself. It is written for the procrastinators, who always seem to find the time to do anything but what they know they should be doing.

It is for the erstwhile lovers of life, those people who feel that they have been separated from the life they love and can't seem to get out of their own way and find the path back to that love and happiness.

It is for those who work hard at life but can't understand why the harder they work, and the more overtime they put in, the less happy they are. The hard workers who are unaware of how to set boundaries and feel their unsympathetic bosses are making them sick.

This book is broken down into easy-to-remember and easy-to-respond-to segments of time maximization across each day that can be followed sequentially or tapped into when it suits.

I have called these segments of time maximization "The "8 E's of Equilibrium." The 8 E's provide the framework for balancing the time you spend away from work and outside the nonnegotiable (unless you are the parent of a newborn or toddler) eight hours you require for sleep and restoration.

If you can spend one hour of your available eight hours of leisure time on each of the 8 E's, then you will experience fulfilment in no time at all.

Working from home has become living at work for many. If you work all the time you work, then you deserve eight hours to do as you please.

This book is the distillation of the expert advice I have been given over many years, the many wonderful experiences I've had with clients, and the lessons I've learned from them and the hundreds of books I have read on mental, spiritual, physical, social, business, and family health.

If you want to stop the clock because you're wasting time and need to start the clock to make the very most of the time you have available, turning your leisure time into treasured time, then start the clock, turn the page, and keep reading.

Time starts *now*!

"All that really belongs to us is time;
even he who has nothing else has that."
—Baltasar Gracian, 17th-century Spanish philosopher

1: ENLIGHTENMENT

The Daily Pursuit of Mental and Spiritual Growth

"He who knows others is intelligent;
he who understands himself is enlightened."
—Lao Tzu, ancient Chinese philosopher

INTRODUCTION

Enlightenment is an awakening of sorts, and so the first thing I would encourage you to do upon awakening in the morning is to engage in an enlightening experience.

When I think of an enlightened person, I think of someone who has a high degree of emotional intelligence. These days, emotional intelligence, or EQ, is regarded more highly than IQ, because IQ tests measure how book-smart a person is, rather than how street-smart they are.

In the sixth edition of *On the Origin of Species*, Charles Darwin writes: "It is not the most intellectual of the species that survives; it is not the strongest that survives; but the species that survives is the one that is able best to adapt and adjust to the changing environment in which it finds itself."

Find yourself on the street and you better work out the rules of the game quickly or you won't survive for long. Find yourself in a highly political work environment and you better work out the power bases, lest you be ousted or stifled in your climb to the top.

Why It Matters

What I am essentially talking about is behavioral flexibility. Your ability to handle what life throws at you requires you to have the bandwidth or headspace to be aware of your response to potentially stressful situations. Stress, I believe, is determined by the degree to which you feel in control or out of control of your life.

Enlightening practices will help create harmony in your headspace, and within you, the necessary calm to be cool under pressure.

"Waiting for enlightenment will not bring about enlightenment."
—Khandro Rinpoche, author of *This Precious Life*

CHAPTER 1:

Growth Mindset

═══════════

"The mind, once stretched by a new idea,
never returns to its original dimensions."
—Ralph Waldo Emerson

There was once a little boy who woke up on his 10th birthday and ran downstairs to open his presents. His father was sitting at the breakfast table reading the paper and said to him: "Son, today I am going to tell you about the birds and the bees."

The little boy covered his ears and stomped up and down, shouting: "No! No! No! Don't tell me. *Stop*!"

His father had known his son to be a calm and well-mannered young boy, so he was quite shocked at his behavior. He put a calming hand on his shoulder and asked what was causing such a reaction.

"Daddy, on my seventh birthday, you told me there was no such thing as the tooth fairy, and I've never got another dollar under my pillow since," the little boy answered. "Then on my eighth birthday, you told me there was no such thing as the Easter Bunny, and chocolate has never tasted the same after that.

"On this very day, one year ago, you told me there was no such thing as Santa Claus, and last Christmas was the worst Christmas Day ever!

"If you are going to tell me today, on my 10th birthday, that grown-ups don't really "*do it*," then what have I got to live for?"

I was, in fact, 10 years old myself when my teacher said to the class on the last day of school, just as we were about to head off for our Christmas holiday break: "Stand up, all those who believe in Santa Claus."

I stood up along with two other boys.

"Sit down Lee, you idiot!" she shouted and then proceeded to tell us all the terrible truth.

I asked my older brother Terry if the nasty teacher's comment was true, and he said: "Shoosh! There is no such thing as Santa Claus, but don't let on to Mum and Dad that you know, or you won't get any presents." That indeed was the worst Christmas ever for me as well.

You see, we all did at some stage believe in the tooth fairy, the Easter Bunny, and Santa Claus.

Many of our earliest beliefs were given to us or taken away from us by our parents, and in many cases, the beliefs we have inherited are those of our great-great-great-grandparents.

A belief is in fact a behavior. You can't say you believe one thing and then behave contrary to your beliefs. Well, you can, and many people do. "I like your Christ," Gandhi said. "I do not like your Christians. Your Christians are so unlike your Christ."

With a growth mindset, you are encouraged to spend time challenging your beliefs. Your beliefs should serve, support, nurture, and sustain you. If they do not, then you need to find what it is you do believe in. There is no growth in the comfort zone. I used to believe men who drank green tea were soft (I now drink two cups a day). I used to think yoga was for hippies (I sometimes find hot yoga tougher than a weights workout). I used to think, believe, and act from a place of a fixed mindset rather than of a growth mindset.

There is a rather apt Mark Twain quote that goes: "It ain't what you don't know that gets you into trouble. It's what you know for sure that just ain't so."

When you set challenges for yourself that encourage you to step out of your comfort zone, that is where growth will occur.

Doing one thing every day that scares you is not about being reckless; it's about doing the things that have held you back in the past. Saying no to a group of friends who invite you out for drinks that will derail your health and fitness goals is part of a developing growth mindset. In contrast, the inner critic—that little voice inside your head I like to call "the mini-me"—will always whisper words of discouragement and try to appease your weaker self.

A client in a CrossFit session once told me that his mind wouldn't let him do one more rep. "Whose mind is it?" I asked. "Tell that mind of yours that we need to keep this body ticking along so that Mr. Mini Me wakes up tomorrow morning."

With a growth mindset, you challenge your beliefs and set your intentions out on the table. That is, you write them down and review them regularly. Each time you have a setback, you adjust the growth plan so that you're better prepared for the future. Then you *make it happen*!

Your growth plan requires you to be honest with yourself.

Life is about meaning and memories. You create the meaning through the memories and the memories through the meaning.

Remember to grow.

> *"Enlightenment is man's leaving his self-caused immaturity."*
> —Emmanuel Kant

CHAPTER 2:

Mood Monitoring

---

*"Emotional self-awareness is the building block of the next
fundamental emotional intelligence: shaking off a bad mood."*
—Daniel Guleman, author of *Emotional Intelligence*

There are many good suggestions around moods and mood monitoring. One is that it is OK to sit with a bad or sad mood. If the mood suits your setting, then run with it, however, if it is going to bring others down with you, then shift it. I call this changing the channel.

I've often said: "Hey, listen, it looks like your mood doesn't really want my company right now, so I'll be off." Up to this point, I will have made a few efforts to help lift the mood, but my carefully chosen words always generate an immediate positive response and an improvement in a person's mindset.

The immediate change also shows me that it is possible to change the channel. The choice is yours as to whether you decide to return to what you were feeling after we have parted company.

I once witnessed a waiter scald herself in a café and quickly put her arm under cold running water. She felt the pain and applied her known remedy. We experience mental pain and rather than apply known remedies, one of which is to change the channel, we continue to watch the bad movie play out.

There are times when I have woken up and felt that the mood I was in was far less than ideal, so I changed it. *Easier said than done*, you might think, but just as a bad mood maintained too long runs the risk of turning into a bad personality, so it is with a good mood.

Given I have been purposefully practicing being in a good mood for many years, I would like to think I now have a good personality. What do I mean by good? A happy personality or a sunny disposition that makes me and those around me happy.

Abraham Lincoln said he believed: "Most folks are about as happy as they make up their minds to be."

One of my first responsibilities of a morning is to receive personal training clients from my mastery program. The aim of the program is to create a superstar mindset and body after 12 weeks, so I can't afford to allow clients to waste a second being distracted by a bad mood. If my client is cranky or miserable, I gradually raise the level of exertion on the treadmill or exercise bike while asking them a few questions.

In most cases, within about 10 minutes, their mood becomes positive. I love the idea that people leave my sessions in a better frame of mind. I'm convinced it is because they have moved their body, which moves their minds. Physiology is psychology. How you feel very much affects how you think. We can control how we feel by what we allow into our thoughts.

The real trick with moods is to catch the mood before it catches you.

When you choose as one of your enlightenment practices to monitor your moods, think about the things that are likely to change your moods or have an immediate effect on them.

When my children were toddlers, I adopted a time management hack that involved not listening to, watching, or reading the news. If the news was newsworthy, I would research it in my own time and go beyond the "Henny Penny, the sky is falling" version that sensationalist mastheads tend to spread. I saved an enormous amount of time, and importantly, my moods were not affected by the vagaries of the news cycle.

It's the best way I have learned to maintain control over the thoughts I allow into my mind.

But the onus is always on us to create our good news and search for the good news stories in our lives.

For example, choose a music playlist that uplifts your spirits. If a song reminds you of an ex-partner, delete it. If you want to monitor your mood, then set it with music, scented candles, your favorite perfume, or aftershave. Eat mood-enhancing foods. Get eight hours of sleep and practice positive thinking.

The first behavior in my morning routine is to have a three-minute cold shower; the very next habit—most usually during my cold shower—is to smile at myself in the mirror for one minute. I heard an Esther "Abraham" Hicks talk once where she said it takes less than 15 seconds for a negative thought to turn into a negative mood but three times as long for a positive thought to become a positive mood. I usually laugh at myself much earlier than one minute, but I am priming myself to be happy and it works.

For an immediate mood-calming experience, physiological sighing, a "do anywhere" breathing technique discovered by doctors in the 1930s, requires you to take one deep breath through your nose with your mouth closed, and immediately upon filling your lungs, one last quick nasal breath to ensure all air sacs are opened, then to exhale slowly through your mouth for as long as you can.

Stress has the effect of collapsing air sacs (alveoli) in our lungs, creating shortness of breath and making us more anxious. By purposefully reopening your alveoli, you are calming both mind and body. It can take as few as one round to experience the immediate benefits of a calmer mood, yet you will enjoy doing up to eight rounds.

As a last resort, consider purchasing a mood ring. The idea is that stress or a bad mood lowers body temperature and takes blood away from the extremities, darkening the ring's color. If you are happy, your body temperature rises, and the ring turns pink or purple. The jury is still out on whether there is any scientific truth behind it, but in the very least, a mood ring reminds you of this important step in achieving enlightenment.

I lost my mood ring years ago and I am still not sure how I feel about that ...

"I, not events, have the power to make me happy or unhappy today.
I can choose which it shall be. Yesterday is dead, tomorrow hasn't
arrived yet. I have just one day, today,
and I'm going to be happy in it."
—Groucho Marx

CHAPTER 3:

Batch Thinking

"It seems to me that the real problem is the mind itself, and not the problem which the mind has created and tries to solve. If the mind is petty, small, narrow, limited, however great and complex the problem may be, the mind approaches that problem in terms of its pettiness."
—Jiddu Krishnamurti

Einstein said you cannot solve a problem with the same thinking that got you into the problem. Batch thinking is the idea of setting time aside in the areas and style of thought required to spark eureka moments that will solve problems and help you gain clarity in murky, confusing, or worrying situations.

Most people only "get" time to think when they are busy doing other things. For example, they might be sitting in traffic thinking about the annoying colleague they are about to encounter at work and the surrounding bottleneck. I often muse that the campfire was the original television for the cave dweller—yet a live fire, as entertaining as it can be, is not as mindless as television viewing can be.

One of my favorite things is to sit in front of a fireplace or campfire and get lost in the flickering flames of thought. I've "fire dreamed" many of the things that I have achieved over the years, and I keep a journal with a red star on the cover to record these dreams in. I set a two-week deadline for acting on these ideas, or I tear the unacted upon idea out of the book. It is a great motivator for action and accountability.

You see, thinking is great if it is followed by action. I feel that if I dwell too long on something then I need to stop dwelling on it and start dealing with it.

"Don't dwell _on_ it—deal _with_ it!" is one of my mantras.

Curiously, about the only thing in life you have complete control over is your thoughts.

But there are two downsides: overthinking and stinking thinking.

Overthinking is the plight of the perfectionist; stinking thinking is the plight of the masochist.

The problem for perfectionists is that nothing is ever perfect, so in overthinking, they struggle to commit or finish the task at hand. The problem for masochists is that stinking thinking keeps them in the status quo, which seems to suit them.

That's probably why Cicero said: "Indecision is the thief of opportunity."

The best way I know of optimizing your thinking is to dedicate set time to deep thought and contemplation. The benefits of allocated thinking time (batch thinking) are that you find your outcome and have eureka moments, rather than carrying thoughts around with you or losing sleep over them.

It was once explained to me that taking time out from a busy period to sit and think for half an hour is like setting a bucket of muddy water down. The liquid eventually settles with the "silt" sinking to the bottom and the rest of the water clearing up. Like a "clearwater revival" of the mind.

I love the line in Peter Pan where Peter says: "You just think lovely, wonderful thoughts, and they lift you in the air." If you are the type of person who finds it difficult to sit still for half an hour without distractions and allow your thoughts to gather, then a half-hour walk or run can have the same benefit. I often wonder whether I am getting an endorphin rush from a half-hour run, or the clarity that I am experiencing after 30 minutes of uninterrupted thought. (I don't run with headphones.)

Set time aside for productive thinking. I set an alarm for 3:00 p.m. every day to think about the things that may keep me awake at 3:00 a.m.—the worrying things I can do nothing about at 3:00 a.m. I know how well I am doing with this proactive batch thinking when my 3:00 p.m. alarm goes off and I have nothing to worry about and can keep getting on with my day.

If you are prone to worry, set aside a one-hour meeting with yourself on a Saturday morning when you can worry to your heart's content. Set a calendar date with yourself for 10:00 a.m. every Saturday and send yourself an email calendar invite with the subject line "WORRY TIME."

During your week, when a potentially worrying thought comes to mind that distracts you from your daily happiness, put it on your worry list.

What you will find over time is that you get a lot more joy out of each day.

Once 10:00 a.m. rolls around on Saturday morning, look at the worry list you have taken with you to the meeting. Now cross off all the things on the list that are completely out of your control and decide to take the first step in dealing with the things you can. Don't dwell on it, deal with it.

Marcus Aurelius put it best when he wrote: "You have the power over your mind, not outside events. Realize this and you will find strength."

Not long into your Saturday morning worry meetings, you will find 80 percent of the things on your worry list don't worry you anymore. "There are more things likely to frighten us than there are to crush us; we suffer more often in imagination than in reality," Seneca said.

Write lists. They act as great reminders and "minutes of the meeting" that you just had with your mind. Lists allow for greater mind space to think on your feet in daily life. Make to-do lists, shopping lists, and repair lists for your Saturday morning worry meeting.

Benjamin Franklin said about an ordered life: "Let all your things have their places; let each part of your business have its time." He also said: "Resolve to perform what you ought, and perform without fail, what you resolve."

Batch thinking gives you space to monitor anxious thoughts about the future as they creep in. Ask yourself, "What is the worst thing that could go wrong in this situation?" Then decide upon all that is in your power to avoid this thing happening and get to work on actioning these steps. In the school of philosophy known as Stoicism, it is expressed by the Latin phrase *premeditatio malorum*, meaning the premeditation of the evils, or troubles that might lie ahead.

The space you choose to batch your thinking in should help you create the thoughts you want to have and the life you wish to manifest. It could be the sauna, the beach, or the garden.

Don't ruminate on anything for longer than 20 or 30 minutes. More than this and stinking thinking will take over. I know people with far too much time on their hands, who create mischief for others and become the trouble-making colleagues we face in the office or workplace. Most political players in the office don't work as hard at their jobs as they do at "the game."

As the Russian novelist Fyodor Dostoevsky said: "To think too much is a disease."

Two things seem to happen with monotonous regularity when I think of a morning: I have an epiphany or an anxious thought.

If I do nothing with the epiphany, nothing good happens. If I do nothing with the anxious thought, nothing bad happens. If I do something with the epiphany, something great happens. If I let the anxious thoughts run amok, I end up worrying for no reason. As Shakespeare said: "For there is nothing either good or bad, but thinking makes it so."

This is also the time to practice mindfulness. All you have is this moment and all you can influence right now is this moment. Focus on this idea today, and every day from now on and played right, you will naturally create a better future and naturally leave a better past.

So, with peace of mind as my highest priority, the morning thinking routine sets me up for a naturally good day.

With batch thinking, be kind to yourself. Positive self-mind talk is so important. Don't allow the voice in your head to speak to you in a way you would not tolerate from another person. Your thoughts become your words, your words become your actions, your actions become your destiny, so speak well to yourself and your future self.

When you sense stinking thinking manifesting in your mind, purposely change the channel to "linking thinking": link your thoughts to your goals and what you do have in life, not what you don't. When you focus on what you have, what you lack disappears. When you focus on what you lack, what you have in life disappears

Of course, there are those of us who try to avoid thinking altogether with distractions such as television, social media, gossip, and addictive vices.

Ironically, I am reminded of a *Simpsons* episode where Bart has taken over the local radio station and Lisa walks into the loungeroom, turns the TV off, and places a radio on top of it.

"People of Springfield, we have an announcement to make!" she declares.

Homer's response is gold: "Well turn something on—I'm starting to think!"

> *"All men's miseries derive from not being able
> to sit in a quiet room alone."*
> **—Blaise Pascal**

CHAPTER 4:

Journaling

"Thinking is the soul talking with itself."
—Plato

We learned to think on paper. I have been encouraging people to journal for years. When I suggested the idea of journaling as thinking on paper to an executive leadership team in a work-life balance workshop, one executive said that he tried journaling but the habit wouldn't take. I asked him how he had been writing down his thoughts and he told me that in the evening, in bed, he would type them into his laptop, the same machine he had moments earlier been finishing the day's work on.

When I put it to him that the idea of writing in a journal or even a notepad was a terrific way to disconnect, he said he was a child of the iPhone generation brought up with iPads and laptops.

"Yet!" I continued. "On your first day of school, the teacher would have put a piece of paper in front of you and given you a lead pencil and asked you to write your name on it, and eventually to write 'The cat sat on the mat,' or 'Digger chased Sam.'"

I pointed out that as he progressed through school, he would have been instructed to fill in his comprehension of a story in written form with a biro, and he would have sat his final exams using either a pen or pencil. His thoughts and education had all been released on paper.

Write your aspirations and commitments down and read them often. Once they are on paper, they are out of your head and into the first stages of action.

The practice of daily journaling is such a cathartic way to start and finish the day.

Early morning journaling helps you narrate a positive plan and can be the written articulation of your goals for the day. I like to freewheel over two A4 pages each morning to sharpen my clarity and improve creativity before I have started to think about anything else.

Evening journaling, apart from expressing gratitude, holds you accountable to the aims you outlined in the morning. It also helps you fall asleep faster by clearing your mind of worry.

Being able to express your thoughts on paper provides more certainty on where you are headed and how far you have come than memory or experience alone can do.

With your *dream* life in mind, adopt an attitude of "action breeds inevitability." If day by day, you do one thing beneficial toward your *dream* life, you will inevitably live the *dream* life you have designed.

A child once asked me: "David, what is a yearn-all?"

I thought he may have overheard me talking to his mother about the benefits of keeping a daily journal and mistaken "yearn-all" for journal. I guessed he was, without knowing it, onto something …

A journal is a tool for planning all the things you yearn for—your *dream* life.

As it turned out, he was asking me, "What is a urinal?" Curiously, a journal can become just that. A tool where, without action, you are just flushing your dreams down the toilet.

The benefits of journaling are cumulative. Whenever I ask clients if they have been practicing physiological sighing, they all say yes, because they feel the positive effects immediately.

They say a problem shared is a problem halved, but sometimes a problem shared can be a problem squared, depending on who you share it with. Think on paper—share your thoughts with your soul, mate!

"You control your future, your destiny. What you think about comes about. By recording your dreams and goals on paper, you set in motion the process of becoming the person you most want to be. Put your future in good hands: your own."
—Mark Victor Hansen, American motivational speaker

CHAPTER 5:

Meditation

═══════

"To sum up the meditative process, you have to break the habit of being yourself and reinvent a new self; lose your mind and create a new one; prune synaptic connections and nurture new ones; unmemorize past emotions and recondition the body to a new mind and emotions; and let go of the past and create a new future."
—Dr. Joe Dispenza, author of *Breaking the Habit of Being Yourself*

Dr. Joe Dispenza's quote not only sums up the meditative process, but it also sums up the reason why most people are scared of meditation. It doesn't have to be this complicated.

Meditation is not sitting on the top of a mountain with legs crossed chanting "om" or the like to the heavens. Meditation is the practice of contemplative thinking or focusing on the breath or a repetitive mantra.

There are opportunities to meditate all around us and we knew this instinctively as children. Lying on the grass gazing up at the sky and looking for animals or shapes from within the clouds is meditative.

Stargazing is meditative. Daydreaming is meditative. Counting reps while exercising is meditative.

To all those who find meditation too hard, I suggest simplifying your meditation practice by setting aside space and time to close your eyes and block out all the noise and pace of your daily life.

The people I have met who don't meditate always tell me that they tried a couple of times, and it didn't do anything for them, or they felt stupid doing it.

Not too dissimilar to the answer people give me about why they are inconsistent with exercise.

If you saw immediate results from exercise, you would stick with it. If you experienced immediate benefit from meditation, you would keep doing it.

I tell people who say they have tried meditation but it didn't work: "It's like quitting the gym because you didn't get big biceps after two visits."

The benefits from meditation aren't so much derived from disappearing from the face of the earth for hours on end but in the catching of the mind as it gets distracted.

So, once you sit or lie down and focus on clearing the clutter from your mind, the thoughts that pop into your head should be put to the side. It is the returning to the thinking of nothing or the focusing only on your breath that builds the mind muscle.

The mind muscle is built just like the muscles of our bodies.

When you lift weights, muscles grow more fibers, and you get bigger and stronger.

When you meditate and catch yourself in the onset of distraction, it is this return to quietude that builds new neural pathways in the brain. Just like a bicep curl.

Neural pathways are how the brain sends signals to itself, and in turn, to all parts of your body. Repetitions of behavior are grooved into the lanes of the brain which form the adoption of habits, good or bad.

I liken the benefits of meditation to peak-hour traffic coming to a standstill at the entrance to a bridge. If the bridge had more laneways, the traffic would flow more smoothly. Once the mind builds new neural pathways, the traffic of stress and other messages being driven in all day long are more easily processed and dealt with because of the extra laneways.

Austrian psychologist Viktor Frankl, author of *Man's Search for Meaning*, wrote: "Between stimulus and response there is a space. In that space is our power to choose our response. In our response lies our growth and our freedom."

The space Frankl speaks of is made more available to us when we have created the time to meditate and build new neural pathways.

Like anything I have learned, I have first sought out the books of instruction in that field, and if a real interest is created, I seek out further education.

I encourage you to look further into meditation, whether you feel that it is working for you or you feel you just aren't getting it. As you would hire a personal trainer in the development and care of your body, investigate learning meditation with an instructor.

Guided meditation with an app works for many; listening to meditative music works for others and is much more cost-effective. Transcendental meditation, which was made popular by the Beatles in the late 1960s, can be quite expensive to learn.

A cost-efficient hack I have been practicing for years is to look for graduates or start-ups offering their services for a fraction of what the experts are charging.

For example, I learned four different practices for meditation over four weeks for less than $150 from a young graduate's start-up business.

There is no more presence-based experience you can create for yourself than meditation. The present, or the "now," is measured as three seconds. All we have is this moment.

Most meditative practices encourage you to think of nothing and focus on your breathing.

My breathwork routine is known as alternate nostril breathing and is my take on *pranayama*, the name for all yoga breathing practices.

Alternate nostril breathing, also known as *nadi shodhana*, is designed to balance the left and right brain in a calming way.

I've adapted this practice to involve picturing the number 8 lying across my eyes, like an eye mask.

Beginning with my right hand, I place my index finger at the center of the 8, my thumb on my right nostril, and my middle finger over my left nostril.

I release my middle finger and breathe in for the count of eight, close my nostril again with my middle finger, hold my breath for the count of eight, and release my thumb from my right nostril, breathing out through my right nostril for the count of eight seconds.

I do this eight times for the left nostril and then eight times for my right nostril.

All the while, I am picturing the number 8 in a continuous flowing pattern—as in the infinity symbol—revolving around my left and right eye sockets with the focus on my breath.

It is exceedingly difficult to think of anything else while picturing the swirling figure 8, a number that is also said to mean equilibrium in numerology.

Prevention is better than cure. You do not preempt anxiety; you prevent anxiety. Sunscreen is designed to prevent sunburn. You only have to apply aloe vera to sunburn so many times before you get the idea that sunscreen should be applied daily. Meditation and breathwork are sunscreen for the mind.

Even if your thoughts wander during meditation, ask yourself why that's happening. Then do something positive toward those thoughts afterward. As a novice, keep a palm card beside your meditative space and write down the recurring thoughts so that once they are on paper, they are out of your mind. Bring them up during your Saturday morning worry meeting if they are of concern. Transfer them from your "to-do" list to your "ta-da!" list once they are done and no longer a concern.

I recommend journaling before meditation for added clarity.

> *"Our fatigue is often caused not by work,*
> *but by worry, frustration and resentment."*
> —Dale Carnegie

CHAPTER 6:

Prayer

---

*"It is better in prayer to have a heart without words
than words without heart."*
—Mahatma Gandhi

This chapter is not designed to push religion upon you. I was brought up a Catholic. I am the middle child of a 10-kid family. Two of my brothers became priests. We attended church for a one-hour long mass at least twice a week, and, led by my father, we prayed the rosary on our knees around the dinner table every night. I served as an altar boy at church every Sunday from the age of 8 until I left home at 18.

Research has shown that people who regularly pray live on average four years longer than those who do not. Prayer is reflective and meditative if you do it, as Gandhi said, "with heart."

The process of meditation is, as already discussed, a very "peace-of-mind" experience. I find prayer very peaceful with similar benefits to meditation.

I have investigated many religions other than the faith I was given. My father's parting words from any phone call or visit were always said with great enthusiasm: "Keep the faith!"

I have faith in God, and I have plenty of evidence of His works in my life.

I have found many ways to pray. First and most common is rote prayer or repetitive prayer, which can feel like a guided meditation. My morning stretching routine is accompanied by rote prayers rather than a timer.

Then there are hymns. In the words of Saint Augustine, "Those who sing pray twice." I love to sing. I once heard a spiritual leader say: "If God gave you a good voice, then sing in gratitude for that voice. If He gave you a bad voice, then sing to get back at Him!"

I find prayer a wonderful verbal articulation of my goals if I'm asking for support, strength, or something I need in life.

Another type of prayer is the prayer from the heart, where you are mindfully communicating with the universe or God. It's the kind of prayer that you may have seen in the movies: "Hey God? Are you there? If you are, I really need your help right now."

It is much like the gratitude you would show to someone who had invited you over for a delightful home-cooked meal. If you show absolute gratitude and delight during the dinner and then call the next day to say thank you once again, there is a good chance that person will invite you back again.

Praying is not wishing. I had been praying for something that I wanted in my life for a few years, when one day I asked the question: "What's going on? I have been praying for this for a few years now."

The response in my mind was: "Are you praying or are you wishing?" I paused for a while and the next words that came to my mind were: "What are *you* doing about this?"

I made a couple of phone calls that day and changed my approach and attitude enormously, and within two weeks, I had *miraculously* received what I had been praying for.

I often remind myself of a saying that I read in Aesop's fables as a young boy, "God helps those who helps themselves":

> "A wagoner was once driving a heavy load along a very muddy way. At last, he came to a part of the road where the wheels sank halfway into the mire, and the more the horses pulled, the deeper sank the wheels. So, the wagoner threw down his whip, and knelt down and prayed to Hercules the Strong: 'O Hercules, help me in this my hour of distress.'
>
> But Hercules appeared to him and said: 'Tut, man, don't sprawl there. Get up and put your shoulder to the wheel. The gods help them that help themselves.'"

When I was 22, I was involved in a boating mishap and thrown into rough seas about two kilometers (1.25 miles) out from shore. I had been fishing with a friend and we had forgotten to drop anchor.

I couldn't swim and I was panicking. It was winter and I was wearing a heavy coat, boots, and jeans and started to sink quickly. I managed to get all my gear off, and my mate, an ex-surf lifesaver, decided to swim after the boat.

My life, as they say, "flashed before my eyes."

I recounted all the things that I had done and achieved in my very short life (I was calming myself with my optimism, right to the end) and had accepted my fate. I then started to think of all the things I still had not achieved. It was very cold, and I was losing body temperature and strength, trying to tread water.

I prayed aloud. I prayed that if I were saved, I would do so much more with my life than I was doing at the time. I said prayers of gratitude for the life I had lived so far and recalled all the good things that had happened to me.

The calmness I felt in the moment spurred me on as I swallowed water and bobbed up and down.

Oh, the promises I made that day …

After what was more than an hour in the sea, my prayers turned to singing hymns through chattering teeth.

Miraculously, the boat had somehow turned itself around and my friend was able to climb aboard and rescue me. He told me later that he fully expected I had drowned and that he was just searching for his LA Raiders jacket, which had cost him $300 in the US. I hope he was joking.

Some of my friends are atheists. They have said that my prayers saved me on some levels. Praying relaxed me, enabling me to focus with a calm mind and reverse the panic process. It meant I could make more sensible decisions to ensure my survival when the boat did arrive. And by reflecting on my life's accomplishments, I was able to reprioritize goals and enhance my drive for survival so that I could have a chance of achieving them.

I know that the prayers I said in those life-and-death moments calmed me down, and the hymn singing kept me warm. It also gave hope that someone might hear me, and my terrible singing.

Was a miracle performed that day? I'm not saying that I walked on water out of that predicament, but I'm here today to tell the story in the hope that you might find some solace in the power of prayer whenever you may need it.

Many religions have different names, shapes, and forms that they give to the God in which they believe.

I would encourage you to believe in something greater than yourself. I would also encourage you to look to all forms of religion or spiritual practice until you find the path or portal to your spiritual enlightenment.

Your beliefs should serve, support, nurture, and sustain you.

If a belief is a behavior, then your beliefs will do all of the above.

If your belief system is one that you inherited at birth and doesn't do any of these things for you, question and explore other spiritual possibilities.

As they say, if you live a very good life and there is no heaven, then you lived a very good life. If you lived a very bad life and there is no hell, then you lived a very bad life.

Bad people aren't happy, which is the reason they behave badly. Good people are happy because they know they are good people.

There are some days I find my yoga session to be more spiritually reviving than any church service or priest's sermon I have ever attended.

Where you find your spiritual nutrition is up to you.

A ship sailing past a deserted island spots a man who has been stranded there for several years. The captain goes ashore to rescue the man and notices three huts …

"What's the first hut for?" the captain asks.

"That's my house," says the castaway.

"What's the second hut for?"

"That's my church."

"And the third hut?"

"Oh, that?" sniffs the castaway.

"That's the church I used to go to."
—Father Kevin Lee from the pulpit on Trinity Sunday

CHAPTER 7:

Earthing

≡≡≡

"Walk as if you are kissing the earth with your feet."
—Thich Nhat Hanh, "the father of mindfulness"

When we talk of someone who has their act together or is in touch with the way the world works, we refer to them as "grounded" or "down-to-earth."

Earthing is connecting with the earth, with nothing between you and it. Standing barefoot on grass is the easiest form of earthing.

The theory and research behind earthing is that the earth's energy or "electricity" is transferred into our bodies and recharges them.

An estimated 1000 to 2000 thunderstorms are happening around the world at any given time, producing as many as 5000 lightning strikes per minute. Lightning involves the transfer of a massive number of negative charges to the ground.

The sun also provides energy to the surface of the earth, which is how circadian rhythms are established.

When you connect bare skin to the earth, a flow of electrons and energy transfers through an electric pathway. The negative ions in the earth combine with the positive ions in your body.

Earthing calms your nervous system, balances cortisol (the stress hormone), improves blood circulation, and lowers blood pressure. It also reduces inflammation, promotes healthier digestion, and delivers a better night's sleep. It may even help you in bed …

Richard Gere's high-flying character in *Pretty Woman* was encouraged by Julia Roberts' carefree character to go to the park and walk barefoot to experience what real life felt like.

Our lives are so disconnected from the planet by shoes, tar, cement, and fluorescent lighting that it doesn't surprise me the countries least concerned about the environment are the developed nations where most of their populations' days are spent sheltered in high-rise buildings with very little access to nature.

To get the full benefits of earthing, you need to spend 20 to 30 minutes of bare-skinned contact with the earth. It's easy and natural. Try activities such as swimming in a lake or the ocean or lying on grass.

The most straightforward benefit of earthing is reliving our childhood. That fantastic time when we ran about barefoot and climbed trees to catch cicadas or built sandcastles at the beach.

"And forget not that the earth delights to feel your bare feet
and the winds long to play with your hair."
–Kahlil Gibran

CHAPTER 8:

Forest Bathing

===

*"There is no Wi-Fi in the forest, but I promise
you will find a better connection."*
–Ralph Smart, author and psychologist

The term *shinrin-yoku* was coined by the Japanese Ministry of Agriculture, Forestry and Fisheries in 1982 and can be defined as *"making contact with and taking in the atmosphere of the forest."*

Forest bathing is pretty much mindful bushwalking. It is the total immersion of all your senses in nature.

Where I think a lot of people go wrong with bushwalking or camping is that they do not practice a very important part of forest bathing, which is digital detoxing.

I am an avid bushwalker. Growing up surrounded by bushland, I have cherished memories of camping with my brothers.

I lost someone very close to me many years ago and was in a state of despair for two days. The only thing on my mind was the memory of the times we had spent together camping, kayaking, and bushwalking and the sad fact we would never experience them again.

On the third day, I tried to escape the melancholy by going for a run in the bush to clear my head.

It was sweltering, so I took off my shirt and ran even faster.

I felt the cooling breeze on my skin. The sounds of every creature that lived in the parkland seemed to drown out the sorrowful thoughts in my mind. It even felt like the cicadas and native birds were following me around the trail.

Normally I receive time lapse and distance announcements from Map My Run or pings from text messages and phone calls from clients when I walk or run this trail. This time, I left the phone at home.

For the first time in many years, it seemed I was present to every sensual experience this natural wonderland had to offer. It began to rain, and I could smell the native wildflowers and even the tree bark.

It was during this time that the word "petrichor" randomly popped into my head.

I had no idea what it meant.

Later that night, as I put aloe vera cream on my sunburn, I looked up the meaning of "petrichor" on dictionary.com. "A pleasant smell that frequently accompanies the first rain after a long period of warm, dry weather," it said.

It was obviously no accident that it had sprung into my mind, because it triggered childhood memories of getting caught in a bushland downpour with my eldest brother Kevin and the fragrant bush scents that came with that memory of that moment in time.

Indeed, it was the news that Kevin had died in a tragic drowning accident overseas that had so devastated me. I was proud to be his brother. He was my first and greatest mentor, and the only other man who truly understood me. We had a similar sense of humor, which forged our strong bond. We also shared a boyish fascination with cicadas. Even as adults, we would ring each other up and croak the first cicada of the season we had caught down the phone, wherever we were in the world at that time.

Forest bathing for me now is the ultimate digital detox. It is, in essence, a walking meditation.

"Walking is the best medicine."
—Hippocrates, the "father of medicine"

CHAPTER 9:

Stillness

═══════

"We spend most of our time and energy in a kind of horizontal thinking. We move along the surface of things ... [but] there are times when we stop. We sit still. We lose ourselves in a pile of leaves or its memory. We listen and breezes from a whole other world begin to whisper."
—James Carroll, American author

I have five favorite words that I like to consider as often as I can.

Forgiveness, purity, courage, persistence, and patience.

Forgiveness is setting the prisoner free and recognizing that prisoner was yourself.

Creative thinker Robert Brault said: "Life becomes easier when you learn to accept the apology you never got."

You also need to forgive yourself before you can continue a healthy relationship with yourself.

Forgive yourself for the understanding you had as a seven-year-old child when your thinking style was developing. Forgive yourself for the limiting beliefs about yourself that your seven-year-old mind accepted as true. Forgive yourself for the FEAR (False Evidence Appearing Real) you accepted about your future.

Acknowledge your growth now as you only accept and believe what is REAL (Real Evidence About Life).

I like the word purity rather than integrity because I find those who preach integrity usually don't have it. If you are pure of heart and full of love, you are pure of intention and considerate of others and how your actions impact them.

Courage is what you need to back yourself in the face of adversity. As Brené Brown said: "We need to be courageous to be vulnerable and we need to be vulnerable to be courageous."

Persistence is the main thing that ensures you keep going through adversity and keep showing up for yourself and everyone else, every single day. My thoughts on it are summed up by Jacob Riis, the 19th-century social reformer: "It is not the first or the last blow of the sculptor's hammer that breaks the marble, but every single one."

Patience is my favorite. "Nature does not hurry, yet everything is accomplished," Lao Tzu, the founder of Taoism, said.

The problem for most people when they embark upon a new course of action is that their motivation soon wanes when the fruits of their initial labors do not turn into fully developed outcomes.

I often joke to my female friends that God teaches women the patience they will require for the raising of their children by making them wait 40 weeks to meet them. (I also say that children become teenagers to wean us off their adorable preteen years.) Patience, now … children come back around eventually.

I love this Mark Twain quote: "When I was a boy of 14, my father was so ignorant I could hardly stand to have the old man around. But when I got to be 21, I was astonished at how much the old man had learned in seven years."

Patience is indeed a virtue, and it is learned and acquired in the moments of stillness. Stillness is a combination of all the practices we have discussed in this section.

Stillness allows you to let the mind wander. It requires awareness. It wants you to notice. And to notice everything.

I love the early hours of the morning. Most of this book has been written at the crack of dawn during the stillness of the awakening of the day.

The stillness of the evening before sleeping is what allows most of us to drift off. Many people miss this because they're watching television or scrolling social media, which means they go to bed late and miss the stillness of the morning.

The dictionary defines stillness as "the absence of movement or sound."

As I sit now, without movement, fortified by noise-cancelling headphones, I am in a state of peace, in the practice of stillness.

"Adopt the secret of nature: her secret is patience."
—Ralph Waldo Emerson

CONCLUSION/EXERCISE

"In this hour Siddhartha ceased struggling with his fate, ceased suffering. On his face blossomed the serenity of knowledge, which no will opposes any longer, knowing perfection, in agreement with the flow of events, with the stream of life, full of compassion, full of sympathy, abandoned to the flow, belonging to unity."
—Hermann Hesse

'd encourage you to adopt each of the practices of enlightenment and learn which one or ones suit you. My suggestion is to start your enlightenment practice with daily journaling. You will find meditation much easier with a clear mind.

How's this for a challenge?

1. Pack a light backpack with water, nuts or fruit, a notepad, and pen, and walk through a national park or your city's central park, taking in all the surroundings and delights of the environment (with your phone switched off or to silent).
2. Take your shoes off and walk barefoot before sitting on the ground.
3. Close your eyes for a few minutes and meditate.
4. Practice infinity breathing: covering one nostril, breathe in for eight seconds, hold for eight seconds, release for eight seconds, repeat eight times. Then switch the inhalation nostril and repeat the process.
5. Focus on what your available senses are telling you.
6. Open your eyes and say a prayer of gratitude to your God or the universe for this wonderful experience.
7. Begin to journal on how you feel and what thoughts have arisen.
8. With your growth mindset, take the time to ponder your worries and notice that they are a million miles away.

"You are here for no other purpose than to realize your inner divinity and manifest your inner enlightenment."
—Morihei Ueshiba, *The Art of Peace*

2: EDUCATION

The Daily Pursuit of Knowledge

"Read, every day, something no one else is reading. Think, every day, something no one else is thinking. Do, every day, something no one else would be silly enough to do. It is bad for the mind to continually be part of unanimity."
—Christopher Morley, 20th-century essayist

INTRODUCTION

When I was around eight years old, I asked my father when it was that we died. A little young to be contemplating mortality, you might say. But my father's reply was as brief as it was wise: "You die the day you stop learning."

A few weeks later, as I tucked myself into bed, I realized I had been clowning about all day long, having been sent out of the classroom for talking yet again, and hadn't learned a single thing I could recall. Fearing the clutches of the grim reaper, I hurried to the loungeroom, picked a random volume of the *Encyclopaedia Britannica* (the Wikipedia and Google of my day), and opened it up on the Kalahari bushmen. I read as much as I could and slept peacefully because I had earned another day on the planet.

The next day the school principal came to our classroom and asked us all to stand up individually and talk about an interesting topic—without any preparation. When it was my turn, I waxed lyrical about the Kalahari bushmen and their nomadic ways, how they caught monkeys by setting traps with rock salt, before setting them free and following them to their fresh water source.

As it turned out, this exercise was a selection process for the school debating team, which I was chosen for. At that moment I recognized I had an excellent recall for facts and figures and could convey these well in spoken format.

It was also in this moment that I developed a passion for education.

> *"Formal education will make you a living;*
> *self-education will make you a fortune."*
> —Jim Rohn

Why It Matters

You don't have to go as far as adopting a *memento mori* (remember you will die) attitude, but know that whatever you know today is all you will know tomorrow unless you educate yourself in the ways of the world and grow in how you view it.

My father wasn't prophesying my death. Over time, I have grown to believe he was probably giving me the child mind's version of "the day you think you know it all is the day you stop progressing."

I've been told, "If you are the smartest person in the room, you are in the wrong room."

Given the greatest promise I make is for you to have the ability to achieve work-life balance by turning leisure time into treasure time, then time spent in the pursuit of knowledge is critical.

"Know thyself" is one of the most profound phrases in human history. No wonder Socrates is best known for it. Self-discipline and time management require an understanding of yourself, how you spend your time, where you value time spent, and where you are wasting it.

The greatest investment I believe anyone can make is the investment in self, and the only constant investment that costs so little is self-education and autodidacticism.

> *"If a man neglects education,*
> *he walks lame to the end of his life."*
> **—Plato**

CHAPTER 10:

Reading

===

*"The man who does not read has no advantage
over the man who cannot read."*
–Mark Twain

Reading is without doubt the greatest gift I have been given.

As a young child, if I had been caught misbehaving at home I was sent to my bedroom, after first being punished by my father.

Now the bedroom of my youth was not the Disneyland that children of today are sent to if they are sent for time-out at all.

Upon being sent to my room and pondering the general unfairness of life, I would pick up a book and get lost in its pages, almost feeling like I was getting away with something. Such was my enjoyment of reading.

I remember one particularly well-behaved day for me, I told my mother I was bored, and she answered, "Boredom is self-inflicted, you can choose a chapter or a chore." I chose a chapter.

American poet Dorothy Parker was more poetic: "The cure to boredom is curiosity. There is no cure for curiosity."

I have great memories of the journeys I have been taken on through the pages of novels, as if they were real events in my life. They have become part of my life's journey.

My first job out of high school was as a mail boy in the Sydney CBD, a 90-minute commute from my home in the Blue Mountains.

I had a good couple of hours available to me each workday to either read a novel or catch up on some sleep.

In the morning I would snooze, but in the evening I would read, looking up from my book at each station along the way, so as not to miss my stop.

One morning, as we pulled into the Central Station terminus, I noticed someone had left behind a book. It was *The Power of Positive Thinking* by Dr. Norman Vincent Peale.

I read it on the way home that day and was inspired by the advice Dr. Peale gave about thinking positively. I started dispensing that advice to my fellow mail boys and any of the receptionists and secretaries I delivered mail to over the next week.

One particular receptionist was very receptive. She was also reading a self-help manual: *The Magic of Thinking Big* by David Schwartz, and we agreed to swap when we finished.

Between the two books I quickly developed a higher level of optimism and greater expectations for myself.

One of them claimed that only five percent of the adult population applied for jobs that were paying over $25,000 a year (a princely sum when the book was written), because in the author's opinion, only five percent of the population believed they were worth that amount.

Energized by this revelation, I sourced the Wednesday newspaper, which carried the weekly employment section, and circled all the jobs paying $25,000 a year.

I applied for all the jobs that didn't require a degree or technical skills and soon scored an interview with a publishing company.

As *The Power of Positive Thinking* and *The Magic of Thinking Big* advised, I asked lots of questions in the interview and suggested the benefits I would bring to the company and the problems I could solve, all in an enthusiastic and engaging manner.

The expectations of the job were outlined to me, and as we came to the end of the meeting I was asked about my age.

"So, you're 19, then I'll start you on $19,000 a year," the publisher said.

"But the job was advertised for $25,000 a year," I protested.

The publisher explained that he had expected candidates would be aged 25 because that's who the job was aimed at. I argued that he'd expect the same workload from me as he would from a 25-year-old, and continued to press him in a positive, big-thinking way.

"You said that if I didn't work out after three months, you would fire me," I reminded him. Then as if by magic, I came up with a proposition: "What if, after three months when—not if!—I have exceeded all your wildest expectations, you put me on that $25,000 a year?"

He said he'd have to write into the contract what those wildest expectations were, and we shook hands on it. Because I believed in myself—thanks to the books I'd been reading—I'd been able to convince a high-powered executive to give me an opportunity.

In my first 12 months with the company, including sales commissions, my salary as an advertising sales executive had increased by 800 percent from my mail boy salary.

"Learners are earners!" I've said to many mentees who have said they have no time to read and are unhappy with their pay grade.

I began reading every self-help book I could get my hands on, and I asked for reading recommendations from much older and wiser people.

By the age of 23, I had launched two new magazines as a national advertising manager in Australia's biggest publishing company.

"Readers are leaders!" my father used to say.

But Ralph Waldo Emerson summed it up best: "If we encounter a man of rare intellect, we should ask him what books he reads." It is highly unlikely that this man of rare intellect will be playing small.

I have been devouring self-help books ever since and recommend you do the same.

If you struggle to pick up the habit, join a book club. Otherwise, read what you love until you love to read.

As the Greek Stoic philosopher Epictetus wrote: "Don't just say you have read books. Show that through them you have learned to think better, to be a more discriminating and reflective person. They are immensely helpful, but it would be a bad mistake to suppose that one has made progress simply by having internalized their contents."

If you are inspired by a self-help book, immediately implement the advice within its pages and start to talk about those learnings with like-minded people.

"The more that you read, the more things you will know.
The more that you learn, the more places you'll go."
—Dr. Seuss

CHAPTER 11:

Teaching

———————

"To teach is to learn twice."
—Joseph Joubert

I've met many people who, like me, read self-help books not only to educate themselves, but also to help others.

I retain a lot of my learnings by communicating them to other people. This helps me refine and reinforce what I have learned. My daughters have been beneficiaries of this process many times over the past 20 years, although they may disagree ...

I was fortunate to meet Bryce Courtney, the South African-Australian novelist and author of *The Power of One*, at a literary luncheon in Sydney shortly after my eldest daughter Annabelle was born in 1999.

I asked him what advice he would give to a new parent teaching their child to read. His answer was brilliant:

"Read to your child every night up until the age they can read. At that point buy them an age-appropriate book and continue reading with them. Then have them read to you. If you encourage your child to read a new book every month from then on, by the time they are 18, they will have received a better education than they are ever likely to receive in school."

I did as he said, and by the time my youngest daughter Madeline was nine years old, she had read all seven Harry Potter novels in less than six months.

Teach your children to read. Teach your children to use their imagination, not have their imaginations taught to them by television or video games.

Bruce Lee said: "Instead of buying your children all the things you never had, you should teach them all the things you were never taught. Material wears out but knowledge stays."

I'm a firm believer that by teaching what you have learned and making it age- or audience-appropriate you will gain a better understanding and perspective of the subject matter.

If you have children, or even if you don't, volunteering to help schoolkids read provides an excellent opportunity for you to teach. I also know many retirees who volunteer their time as ethics teachers in schools or speak at men's and women's homeless shelters, teaching the many life lessons they have learned.

"For of those to whom much is given, much is required."
—John F. Kennedy

CHAPTER 12:

Learning

══════════════

"Learning is the only thing the mind never exhausts,
never fears, and never regrets."
—Leonardo da Vinci

After leaving home, I moved into a one-bedroom, ocean-view apartment and lived on my own for three years. It was a big step-up from daydreaming.

My biggest weekly expense was rent. To maintain a lifestyle, I saved money by not spending big on necessities.

I would drink beer at Returned Service Leagues (RSL) clubs where a schooner (425ml/14.3oz) was half the price of the beer a trendy bar and the members were three times the age of my peers. I took out a membership at an old, unfashionable gym where the creaking clientele were similarly old and unfashionable. Some even had hip replacements.

But I gained amazing benefits—and not just financial. At the RSL, I would sit and listen for hours to older men and women tell their war stories and regale me with tales of their successes and failures.

Some of the men at my clifftop gym were connected to colorful racing and underworld identities so I learned the art of appearing ignorant and remaining silent.

I also learned the finer points of conversation and how to speak with people who had completely different life experiences.

And I became a great believer in the conversational and contemplative value of saunas.

The best sauna advice I received was delivered by men who were happy, lean, and spritely. The naysayers were the overweight middle-aged guys who were forever blaming the world or their ex-wives for their lot in life. They weren't in the sauna because they'd exercised hard, they were there because they were sweating off hangovers.

I was, in a way, being educated by people who knew where life's potholes were. Their nuggets of wisdom have lasted to this day.

Those experiences taught me the art and value of listening. It takes great patience to listen, and a genuine interest in the person you are engaging with.

And if you find reading laborious, listening via any kind of audio tech might suit you more.

I used to treat my car like a mobile university and listen to self-help CDs on the way to work.

I also discovered that if you don't care to collect framed diplomas or certificates (no one has ever asked to see any of mine), then voice-recorded university courses save you having to submit anything but your time and attention.

Sales from online courses are tipped to exceed $300 billion in revenue in 2023. In fact, I have created an online course for the 8 E's, specifically to cater to dedicated non-readers who may best learn via video or sound.

These days, I'm a big fan of listening to podcasts in the car. While I'm at the gym, I will put on podcasts or audiobooks on Audible, and I use the Blinkist app as a quick reference point for upcoming books. Blinkist is very useful because it gives a synopsis and breaks things down chapter by chapter.

Audible helps me make the most of a long drive, and on the occasions that I can't put a book down, I download its audio version and pick up where I left off in the car. I find myself looking forward to those long drives because they are a great opportunity for learning.

The greatest way to retain a book's most important contents is by listening to the audio version as well as reading the written version.

"As long as you live, keep learning how to live."
—Seneca

CONCLUSION/EXERCISE

"By three methods we may learn wisdom: first by reflection, which is noblest; second by imitation; which is easiest, and third by experience, which is the bitterest."
—Confucius

Deep learning in and around subjects of particular interest is available to anyone who owns a smart phone.

Don't be satisfied with a lack of knowledge in areas where you feel you should be knowledgeable.

At our fingertips we have Wikipedia, Google, Safari, Microsoft Edge, Bing, and countless other knowledge portals to learn from and to study the world.

You may even find that in pursuit of learning, you uncover a subject you love but were previously unaware of. You will also find that closed doors begin to open. That is the beauty of learning.

Here is my challenge for you:

1. Ask someone who knew you as a child what you told them you wanted to be as a grown-up.

2. When you find this out, if you're not doing just that, investigate an online course for this field of interest and complete it.

3. I doubt very much that this is the first self-help book you have ever read, so I ask you to first *finish reading this book*! Then go to your bookshelf and complete the self-help books you have started but never finished.

4. Set aside a regular time for reading. It doesn't have to be self-help literature. It can be material within the field of your employment, which will improve the understanding of your industry, or a novel, which will enhance vocabulary and creativity.

5. If you're not a reader, download the Audible app or explore podcasts and type in the subject of your fancy. Choose your guru and get hooked.

6. Think of things you wanted to study but didn't, and go online and research what time and money it will take. If it's a three-year degree, then consider this:

in three years' time, you are going to be three years older anyway. Do you want to be three years older with or without the degree and smarter or not?

7. Load the YouTube app on your smart TV and start watching what interests you from an educational perspective. Similar content will then be curated for you.

8. Seek out older and wiser people (they are closer and more accessible than you think) and ask them for advice. Ask them about their life experiences. *And listen.* There is no greater library than an octogenarian's mind.

There is nothing I like better than conversing with aged men. For I regard them as travelers who have gone a journey which I too may have to go, and of whom I ought to inquire whether the way is smooth and easy or rugged and difficult. Is life harder toward the end, or what report do you give it?"
—Plato

3: EXERCISE
The Daily Pursuit of Physical Health and Longevity

"No man has the right to be an amateur in the matter of physical training. It is a shame for a man to grow old without seeing the beauty and strength of which his body is capable."
—Socrates

INTRODUCTION

As early as I can remember I would wake up in the morning to either of two sounds: the clipping of a skipping rope on cement or the hum of an exercise bike.

These sounds were the warmup component of my father's early-morning exercise plan. He would perform a bodyweight routine called the "5BX plan," five basic exercises designed for the Royal Canadian Air Force.

We didn't ever own a car while I lived at home, so for the first 18 years of my life I walked or ran everywhere.

I ran for trains; I ran for buses, and I ran for my life from bullies and the many unleashed neighborhood guard dogs.

We were known as the "Lee Tribe," visibly nomadic, because as a family we walked the five-kilometer (three-mile) round trip to and from the town center.

The bullies picked on us because we were easy pickings.

Coming home from high school, my eldest brother Kevin was beaten up by a gang of youths with chains wrapped around their knuckles.

From that day forward, he vowed to build up his body so that he could protect himself from thugs. He wanted a physique like Lou Ferrigno (the original Hulk) or Arnold Schwarzenegger (Conan the Barbarian and The Terminator), the bodybuilding stars of the time.

He fashioned weights from anything he could because we weren't flush with money. He filled old vacuum cleaner rods with dirt and sand and used bricks as makeshift dumbbells. Kevin was my hero, so it wasn't long before I followed him into weightlifting.

As one of six brothers, I learned how to fight from an early age, and with a short-tempered Irish father, I learned how to duck and weave along the way as well …

Now I'm a qualified boxing instructor, and boxing is still my favorite form of cardio training.

I was fortunate enough to be trained by the great Johnny Lewis for a charity corporate boxing event. The legendary Sydney coach of six world boxing champions told me: "Your only opponent is yourself." It was wise advice. It helped me control my emotions and any temper I may have had.

My father was a huge influence.

"Your health is your wealth," he often said. I believed in those words so much I had them printed on my first personal trainer business cards.

You can have all the money in the world but if you're looking at it from a dialysis machine, what good is it?

"There are no pockets in a shroud" is an old Arabic saying, and I often ask people if they have ever seen a removalist truck following a hearse in a funeral procession.

Training and preparation are everything if you want a fit body and mind.

I always ask my clients their fighting weight, meaning the weight they feel their fittest and healthiest at, and how they can go about achieving it.

I once watched a lethargic heavyweight championship boxing match, and after the fight, which lasted the whole 12 rounds, both fighters complained that they only had three months to prepare.

Neither fighter had a day job as an accountant or a doctor or the like, so I wondered what they were doing with their time outside of the ring? Why hadn't they prepared properly?

How you prepare is how you perform.

I remember hearing a client holding the pads asking his partner not to hit so hard. But the idea of training is to find your maximum resistance so that you know what you can withstand and how you can improve on it.

> "If you knew you had to fight to save your life tomorrow,
> would you change your training today?"
> —Bruce Lee

Why It Matters

A British study of gym members conducted in 2007 found that merely the thought of going to the gym increased a person's positive mental attitude by 28 percent.

After starting a workout, that positive mental attitude increased by a further 62 percent. And post-workout, it had risen another 84 percent. Compelling evidence of the dramatic effect exercise has on the mind.

"Wow, I really regret that workout!" said no one ever.

Depression is more prevalent in our society these days, and we deal with it with prescriptions for anti-depressants and scripts of medication that last months. Patients are asked to give these prescriptions at least six months before they are reexamined, and I wonder: is that just too long to decide whether they are working or still necessary?

I'm a qualified mental health first-aid provider. I know some people are genetically predisposed to anxiety and depression, and I am also very aware that events outside of our control can cause people to feel sad and uncertain about their lives.

My highest priority is peace of mind for myself and the people I am helping. Throughout the day I ask myself: "Will what I am doing bring me peace of mind?"

I suggest to clients who are trying to find out whether they have clinical depression to ask their doctor what the alternative to medication might be.

Before the invention of cholesterol and blood pressure-lowering drugs, doctors would have advised patients to eat less and exercise more.

And before drugs such as Zoloft or Xanax, the main remedy available would have been cold water therapy, exercise, and diet.

I guarantee your doctor today will tell you that staying active and eating well are crucial to your well-being.

I love Wayne Field's nursery rhyme: "The best six doctors anywhere, and no one can deny it, are sunshine, water, air and rest, exercise, and diet."

My "power word" for healthy living is:

LEANER
Less
Eating
And
Normalize
Exercise
Routines

As far as lifespan goes, people who fear aging wouldn't be so fearful of the prospect if they knew that in their 80s and 90s, they could do almost as much as they could in their youth.

And they can. You can train your body and adopt a lifestyle so that it sees you through every life stage. When you look at your lifespan as your health span, you look at your lifestyle more seriously.

For example, the humiliation of being helped up and down from a toilet in your later years can be avoided by incorporating air squats in your exercise routine now.

A client once said to me: "Wouldn't it be great if we had a crystal ball."

Looking at our parents is like looking into a crystal ball.

How they turn out is how you could be. You can either repeat the sins of the father, or right the wrongs of the mother, or follow in their footsteps, if they walk.

The long-term benefits of an exercise routine are self-explanatory. One day you will be 85. Do you want to be 85 with muscularity, morbidity, or mortality?

I have a future pacing exercise that I like to take my clients through. It's based around a mathematical calculation of where you are at in life right now. I start by asking if they have ever imagined what they would look and feel like delivering a speech at their 85th birthday party. Most never have.

As **muscularity** 85-year-old you, you are standing up straight and strong, having risen from your chair unaided, and thanked your loved ones for attending, proud of the memories and experiences you have created and grateful for the loyal friends and family in attendance.

As **morbidity** 85-year-old, you have been wheeled into the general area of a nursing home or respite facility, your breakfast was literally spoon-fed to you, you are riddled with health ailments and unable to speak for the room to hear. But one thing is certain: those in attendance are probably there to ensure their names are included in your will. Where there's a will, there's a relative ...

As **mortality** 85-year-old you, well, you didn't make it.

Using 85 as a benchmark, I ask you to calculate as follows.

85 years equates as 365 x 85 = 31,025 days.

So, if you are 50, 50 x 365 = 18,250 days, leaving you with 12,775 days remaining on the planet till you make 85.

If you are 40, 40 x 365 = 14,600 days, leaving 16,425 days left in your life.

If you are 30, 30 x 365 = 10,950, leaving 20,075 days on the planet and 55 winters. For those who choose to hibernate, remember that summer bodies are made in winter ...

Calculate how many days you have remaining.

The idea of your days being numbered really starts to sink in after this exercise. It makes you seriously consider the value you are placing on your time and your approach to your longevity, i.e., your health span—the active life in your years.

Travelers have all heard the preflight instructions from flight attendants to fix their own oxygen masks before fixing their children's. The first time I paid attention to this directive, I had both of my then toddler daughters either side of me and I thought for a millisecond how I would certainly help them first, before realizing I am not best placed to look after anyone until I am best placed by looking after myself.

"Do the simple things well," my father often said to me as a youngster.

In my selfish teenage years, my father would rebuke me, saying: "As long as number one is alright, hey Davey boy?"

My post-workout smoothie and the recipe I send to my clients is quite simple and is called my "Looking-after-Number-One Shake." Anything done for the benefit of your health isn't selfishness, it is self-preservation. Self-preservation isn't selfishness. It is the confident assurance that we are in control of our own lives to better serve the lives of our loved ones and those around us.

Simply put, starting each day with the goal of self-preservation creates long-lasting physical and mental health benefits.

The idea that saving our own lives is a complex list of things to do creates the fiction that starting is harder than remaining inert.

In the theme of saving your own life or someone else's, could you:

- Run 10 km (6 miles) for help in under one hour?
- Swim 1 km (0.6 miles) to shore in the case of a boating accident?
- Deadlift your own body weight to carry someone out of a burning building?
- Perform 10 chin-ups to climb out that same burning building?
- Bench press your body weight to fend off an attacker?
- Carry your partner or child out of the bush if they've broken their leg or been bitten by a snake?

My approach to life for quite some time has been that of a preventative hypochondriac. My daily to-do list is designed to stop bad things happening to me in the long term. Prevention is better than cure.

It's life's little accidents that chip away at our health in older life. You don't become clumsy. Lack of muscle from inactivity inhibits your footfall speed and makes you unable to catch yourself as you trip. If you break a hip in the process, it is because your bones lack the density of a well-developed hip bone. In turn, a porous osteoporotic hip enables gangrene and other infections to take hold, rendering any exercise impossible.

It becomes like a medical pile-on; one poor health choice begets another.

One in three adults aged 50 and over dies within 12 months of suffering a hip fracture. Don't be one of them.

"Anatomy is destiny."
–Sigmund Freud

CHAPTER 13:

Low Intensity

―――――

"Slow and steady wins the race."
—Robert Lloyd, poet

I have read that you should find a doctor around the same age as you and grow old together. I'm a big fan of my doctor and I follow his directions because I can see he is fit and healthy, and he preaches what he practices.

I visit him every three months to get my full blood tests done and discuss my lifestyle.

Each year, I undertake what I call a winter survival program. For charity and cause awareness, across winter I run or walk 100 kilometers (62 miles), average 100 daily push-ups, and stay off alcohol for "Dry July." I seek sponsors and donations, which keep me honest, and avoid the winter blues—and extra kilos.

When I told my doctor of my running plans, he had a warning: "If you run every day, you might find you'll have difficulties walking when you're 60, but if you walk every day, you'll find you can walk every day in your 90s."

As I prefer a solid, muscular build, the jarring nature of running puts a lot of pressure on my joints.

So, running smaller distances of five kilometers (3.1 miles) or less once or twice a week works best. And I usually incorporate jogging or sprinting into my exercise routines when I'm feeling tubby or down in the dumps.

Walking, however, is my preferred low impact style of training from a mental and cardiovascular perspective.

I've met two Australian prime ministers in my time and, of course, I was curious about what processes they had put in place to handle the toughest job in the country. The older of the two, John Howard, walked early every morning of his 11-year prime-ministership, and continues with that practice into his 80s. It was critical to his physical and mental health and gave him important time to reflect on the day ahead.

The younger man, Tony Abbott, was arguably the fittest politician of all time. He has competed in an Ironman triathlon and run a marathon. He explained to me that there were rarely any political crises before 5:00 a.m., so he rose at 4:30 and rode a bicycle around his neighborhood or parliament house when parliament was sitting. He would also exercise at 3:00 a.m. if he was required to be on an early flight, catching up on sleep in transit.

The cardiovascular system is in a prime state for building between the ages of 10 and 13. If you feel you missed the boat, you've made it harder (but not impossible) to attain peak cardiovascular performance later in life.

As the Chinese proverb goes: "The best time to plant a tree was 20 years ago, the next best time is now."

Low-intensity steady state (LISS) cardio is a great fat-burner if performed on an empty stomach in the morning after completing the Enlightenment and Education plans I have outlined in earlier chapters.

You need between 45 and 60 minutes, and if like I said, you do it on an empty stomach, it will ensure you are burning stored body fat rather than glycogen or carbohydrates from recently eaten food.

LISS cardio is best performed at a level where you could still hold a conversation but would be unable to sing a song.

Between 50 and 70 percent of your maximum heart rate is what you're aiming for.

Your maximum heart rate is 220 minus your age.

"If it's measurable, it's manageable," I like to say, so invest in a heart rate monitor so you can keep yourself honest.

But beware of step counters that only give estimates of your activity and are often off by a factor of 10 to 20 percent.

LISS cardio is less high impact on the body and joints and is perfect for beginners or for someone rebooting exercise routines.

Apart from walking, other good LISS cardio activities are lap swimming, road cycling, kayaking, rowing, cycling and elliptical machines, yoga, golf, and the Stairmaster.

Any form of abdominal or core exercises also work well without breaking longer than 30 seconds between activities.

LISS benefits you in the moment in terms of fat loss and has long-term life benefits.

Many bodybuilders use LISS to create a calorie deficit, without sacrificing muscle mass, to decrease body fat.

The beauty of any exercise routine is that whatever shape you are in and however you got there, the time it will take you to get back to optimum health and physical condition is nowhere near as long as the time it took you to get out of condition. You simply must normalize exercise routines.

"Don't watch the clock; do what it does. Keep going."
—Sam Levenson

CHAPTER 14:

Medium Intensity

"Nothing lifts me out of a bad mood better than a hard workout on my treadmill. It never fails. To us, exercise is nothing short of a miracle."
—Cher

Medium-intensity steady state cardio (MISS) is any exercise routine that is up and down, so to speak, over the course of your 45- to 60-minute workout with a heart rate range between 60 percent and 80 percent of your maximum.

MISS cardio is the most popular form of cardio and burns significantly more calories than LISS.

It will benefit individuals who want to boost endurance and release endorphins. It is fantastic for long-term health and a great stress reliever.

An example of MISS is Fartlek running. (*Fartlek* is Swedish for "speed play.") You run quicker than you normally would, then drop back to a slower pace, but continue to run without stopping. It's ideal if you want to want to be able to run 5 kilometers (3.1 miles) in 30 minutes (10km/h, 6mph) or less.

Another example of MISS is bodybuilding or weightlifting, when your number of reps range from 8 to 12 for each movement and sets are performed 3 to 5 times.

This form of weightlifting is called hypertrophy training, which has the aim of growing muscle.

If you do this style of training two to five times a week, you will have more muscle, a higher metabolism, and burn more fat.

Muscle grows when it is resting. It will not grow if you keep hitting the same muscle every day, so wait 48 hours before targeting that same area again.

My favorite MISS training is compound weightlifting—upper and lower body movements paired together. This style of training is known as peripheral heart action training (PHAT), or shunting. It shunts blood from the upper body to the lower body, making the heart work harder and providing more long-term health benefits.

Compound lifts use more than one muscle group. The best examples are deadlifts, bench press, squats, and chin-ups.

I like shunting sessions. I prefer a one-hour (including a 5- to 10-minute warmup) full body workout with dumbbells or a barbell three to four times a week.

My warmup will be either five minutes on the rowing machine or five minutes of the workout I intend to do using weights one quarter in size.

I recommend that everyone keep a set of dumbbells in their home.

An example of a weights session which can be done at home with dumbbells or in a gym with a barbell would be:

1. Bent-over row
2. Deadlift
3. Biceps curl
4. Squat with weight on shoulders
5. Overhead shoulder press

I will complete these in a sequence or singularly. I do 10 bent-over rows, followed by 10 deadlifts, 10 cleans or 10 bicep curls, 10 squats, and 10 overhead presses. It's done without rest, and I time how long it takes.

The beauty of this workout is that it is scalable. For a client, I adjust the weight to the individual's strength, or fitness levels. It's not a one size fits all, it's a one style fits all.

My oldest client is in her 70s and my youngest client was 14 when he trained with me to make the school rowing team, which he did. A male university student aged 19 performed the same routine above as the septuagenarian does. She does the routine with dumbbells between 4kg and 8kg (9lb and 18lb) while the 19-year-old did it using a 40kg (90lb) barbell.

I also have a "shredding for the wedding" program I take engaged couples through. They train side by side, doing the same workout as each other, but with different weights.

But women needn't fear they will be putting on too much muscle or appearing masculine, as this style corrects weight level and tones muscles. It doesn't bulk them up.

MISS exercise can also include mountain biking, rucking (walking with a weight vest or heavy backpack), moderate intensity skipping, swimming, Pilates, and yoga.

But whatever you do, do it now and consistently. Consistency is another word for patience and inconsistency is another word for impatience.

"Each step forward, no matter how small,
is one step less that has to be taken."
—Larry Riley

CHAPTER 15:

High Intensity

═══════════

"Everyone has a plan until they get punched in the face."
—Mike Tyson

There are no shortcuts in life but these days everyone wants instant results and rewards. This kind of blinkered thinking filters through to exercise routines.

Shortcuts in training almost inevitably end up feeling like a punch in the face. Injury is guaranteed.

High-intensity interval training (HIIT) is anaerobic training that builds up lactic acid in the muscles.

Anaerobic means without oxygen, whereas aerobic means with oxygen.

An aerobic exercise routine is when your muscles have enough oxygen to produce the energy needed to perform the activity.

An anaerobic exercise routine is where the demand is greater than the oxygen supply and you can't keep up with the energy your body is demanding. This leads to lactate production and ultimately the need to stop what you are doing altogether for a period of recovery time.

Sprinters can usually only run flat out for around 7 to 10 seconds.

HIIT exercise routines are performed in short bursts of intense effort for between 5 and 30 seconds at 90 to 100 percent of your maximum heart rate, followed by rest until your heart recovers.

The major benefits are an increased metabolism beyond your exercise routine. This is known as metabolic conditioning.

HIIT is so intense that you run the risk of short-term pain for long-term pain.

With LISS and MISS (aerobic), the fat-burning benefits are limited to the time expended during the exercise routine. But the hits keep coming with HIIT through what is known as excess post-exercise oxygen consumption (EPOC). Your body will burn fat for up to 38 hours after your session is complete in what is known as the afterburn effect.

HIIT is a fast-paced weight loss choice but is also a physiotherapist's dream. I recommend you thoroughly warm up beforehand and stretch afterward.

HIIT burns more fat for less time expended than LISS or MISS but should be incorporated into your LISS and MISS exercise routines no more than twice a week. I would also suggest that your HIIT day is before a rest day, which I think should be once a week.

My favorite HIIT exercise routines are Tabata, boxing, kettlebell swings, and skipping rope.

Tabata training was discovered by Japanese scientist Dr. Izumi Tabata. It runs as follows: 20 seconds on and 10 seconds off for only 4 minutes (8 rounds), which can be 20 seconds of high intensity activity such as burpees, skipping rope, rowing, sprinting, swimming, or hitting a punching bag. I like to incorporate them at the very end of a workout just prior to stretching.

Four ideal TABATA workouts would be:

- 4 minutes of push-ups (8 rounds at 20 seconds on, 10 seconds off)
- 4 minutes of air squats (8 rounds at 20 seconds on, 10 seconds off)
- 4 minutes of burpees (8 rounds at 20 seconds on, 10 seconds off)
- 4 minutes of mountain climbers (8 rounds at 20 seconds on, 10 seconds off)

Add the above together in a workout, and in just 16 minutes, or just over one percent of your day, you have a phenomenal HIIT workout.

The point is not to cause you stress but "eustress." Eustress is defined as beneficial stress—either psychological, physical, or biochemical. It is the good stress our bodies experience because of the aftereffects of exercise.

Simply put, your body will benefit from you picking up heavy things and putting them down again safely for between 30 to 45 minutes, three to four times a week. It will also get a boost from walking between 45 minutes and 60 minutes the other three days a week, leaving one day for rest.

I like the meditative aspect of counting reps because it takes my mind off any pain I might be feeling. That said, don't fixate on numbers. Muhammad Ali was asked how many sit-ups he did in a day and he answered: "I don't count the sit-ups. I only start counting when it starts hurting because they're the only ones that count. That's what makes you a champion."

You must choose something that works for you, but choose something. Choose life. Choose health. Choose longevity. Choose health span.

"I hated every minute of training, but I said don't quit.
Suffer now and live the rest of your life as a champion."
—Muhammad Ali

CHAPTER 16:

Healing

═══════════

"Healing is a matter of time, but it is sometimes
also a matter of opportunity."
–Hippocrates

Time out from exercise routines for the purposes of recovery and healing can be as important as time put in.

You can't pour from an empty cup, and as much as looking after yourself is filling your cup, not taking time away to focus on the healing nature of exercise through recovery practices can be a big mistake.

I often say to my clients that you know you're burning the candle at both ends when the candle won't light.

The "burning the candle at both ends" idiom originally meant that you were burning through your wealth because candles were expensive, and if you were burning them at both ends, you were being wasteful.

These days it is often used to caution against excessive work and to remind us of the importance of a healthy work-life balance to avoid physical and mental exhaustion.

Overtraining for the body is akin to overthinking for the mind. Setting aside one hour a week for a worry meeting with yourself clears the mind and wards off stress, while setting aside an hour for healing your body clears it of accumulated waste and traumas, helping to ward off injury.

The term "psychosomatic" refers to feelings manifesting in the body, such as when an angry person's blood pressure rises in response to their anger.

Somatic psychology is a form of thinking that investigates the opposite idea: that the body affects the way the mind operates. Remember as a teenager when something as simple as the arrival of a pimple could throw your mind into a tailspin?

Physiological sighing introduced in Chapter 1 (one deep breath through your nose with your mouth closed and immediately upon filling your lungs, one last quick nasal breath to ensure all air sacs are opened, then exhaling slowly through your mouth for as long as you can), whilst extremely beneficial in enhancing a positive mood, is also brilliant for commencing the recovery process after exercise, especially HIIT. You immediately move your body from the fight-and-flight stage of training to the rest-and-relax stage of recovery.

Injury and body aches can make an otherwise healthy person feel sluggish rather than full of vitality. As you can think yourself well, you can also think yourself unwell.

Inactivity and lethargy can lead to self-doubt and self-loathing. Adopting a balanced exercise routine can instill levels of confidence and self-assuredness that are unattainable any other way.

I used to say fitness is the payoff of vanity. I've since upgraded my observation. The biggest payoff of fitness is sanity.

One of the main problems people experience when they embrace a health and wellness campaign is that they jump into it with enormous enthusiasm, but the plan goes south because they suffer an injury that derails their momentum.

Proper recovery will help reduce the chance of injury.

My regular go-to form of recovery is, as I mentioned in a previous chapter, the sauna. While I have experienced traditional Finnish style water on coals sauna, I prefer the far infrared sauna, which instead of heating the air, heats the body directly, resulting in deeper tissue penetration but avoiding the extremely hot air of a traditional Finnish sauna, meaning I can stay in for longer.

Full-spectrum infrared saunas detoxify the body of accumulated waste and promote better sleep. They are also a great de-stresser and aid in weight loss—mainly water weight initially—and can burn as many as 600 calories in one hour. Relief from muscular and joint pain such as arthritis is another benefit.

Modern far infrared saunas come with speakers and Bluetooth connections, which if you're smart, you will connect to a meditation soundtrack or a smart audiobook.

Sweating also causes the brain to release endorphins, our natural feel-good chemicals.

Hippocrates said: "Give me the power to create a fever and I shall cure any disease."

I put the fact that I rarely get sick down to the experience of fever-like symptoms each day I have a sauna. I will have a cold shower intermittently while having a sauna, which has been shown to increase white blood cells, which in turn can help boost the immune system and fight off infections.

But when you lose a lot of fluid, always make sure you rehydrate to the point of having light-colored urine.

It goes without saying that the ultimate form of recovery is sleep.

A nonnegotiable eight hours of sleep is required every day.

For those people who believe that sleeping less than eight hours a night is a badge of honor, consider that six hours of sleep is just 75 percent of your required eight hours. Seventy-five percent of your 85-year health span turns out to be just under 65 years. The retirement age is 65.

You work all these years compromising your sleep and leisure time for your job, and when you finally get to retire and enjoy the fruits of your labor, you are either retired permanently or left with the only fruits of your labor being sour grapes or a diet of mashed bananas and prunes.

Wake up to yourself and focus on sleep.

> *"Lack of activity destroys the good condition of every human being, while movement and methodical physical exercise save it and preserve it."*
> —Plato

CONCLUSION

"That one wants nothing to be different, not forward,
not backward, not in all eternity. Not merely bear what is necessary,
still less conceal it .... But love it."
—Friedrich Nietzsche

A *mor fati* is a Latin expression that roughly translates as a "love of fate."

Accept that one day you will die, but the idea is to die feeling young at a very old age.

Rather than waiting for the axe to fall or assuming that your mortality is predetermined, play an active role in your longevity.

"Let fate find us prepared and active," as Seneca said.

After my first 10 years of coaching, I found that most of my clients' mental stresses could be reduced by the inclusion of an exercise routine. I began coaching clients outdoors, incorporating long walks and boxing training. I gained accreditation as a personal trainer and started writing out exercise routines for my clients to do in their own time. Positive physical change is much more evident than positive mental change, as it is visible on the scales, felt in your clothing, and commented on by close friends.

I met a PT with publishing connections along the way, and we co-authored the book *The Complete Health Series*. Once published, I approached *Australian Men's Fitness* magazine to have it featured and was offered the role of commercial director when they learned of my media background.

Serendipity smiled on me when I became the in-house personal trainer at the magazine for six years. During this period, I was exposed to every style of training protocol, equipment, supplement, and apparel that existed in the fitness industry. I continued to chase qualifications and took instructor courses in MMA, UFC, boxing, CrossFit, and kettlebell training.

I met world champion athletes across every imaginable sporting discipline, and even met my childhood hero Arnold Schwarzenegger, who featured on the front cover of the magazine.

The common terminator, I mean *determinator,* with these athletes' success was drive. You must back yourself and be consistent.

The World Health Organization's guidelines for physical activity recommend you do either 150 minutes of moderate or 75 minutes of vigorous activity per week.

If you aim to be active for at least six days a week, 30 minutes a day, or one hour a day five days a week, plus recovery, you will achieve this.

Before you start working out, get a health check-up and devise a plan with realistic goals. Then make exercise a habit by prioritizing it in your daily routine.

"The resistance that you fight physically in the gym and the resistance that you fight in life can only build a strong character."
—Arnold Schwarzenegger

EXERCISE

"And in the end, it's not the years in your life that count.
It's the life in your years."
—Abraham Lincoln

There was a Mercedes Benz advertisement on television many years ago that suggested it would be better if we were born old:

> Life should be the other way around: you should be born old, spend your first years resting, see your aches and pains disappear, start working as the boss, be under less pressure, make fewer, fewer decisions, then, when you're in the prime of your life, buy a Mercedes C class. Have fun—thank you.

It reminded me of F. Scott Fitzgerald's *The Curious Case of Benjamin Button*. If you were born backward, how would you live your life differently?

How's this for some born-backward insights?

1. I would encourage you to apply for life insurance then work backward like Benjamin Button.
2. Find out whether the questions that are asked of you would make you a safe bet.
3. If you answer yes to "Do you smoke?" then quit smoking. Quit doing immediately any of the answers you fail the test on.
4. If you answer no to "Do you exercise regularly?" then start exercising.
5. You'll be asked if there is a history of heart disease in your family. Do everything in your power to avoid dying of a heart attack.
6. Determine what lifestyle changes you now need to make and include them in a letter to your 85-year-old self, as a letter of kindness in a contract: "Dear me, today I made the commitment to us to make the following lifestyle changes and I want you to thank me in our 85th birthday speech and name these lifestyle tips for our grandchildren who will be listening and no doubt recording them on their hologram devices."

7. Write a list of the top five strategies to ensure you exercise every day. This way the kids will listen and so will you. Everybody wants simple tricks these days.
8. Move like children do. Play!

"We don't stop playing because we get old,
we get old because we stop playing."
—George Bernard Shaw

4: EATING

The Daily Pursuit of Nourishment

"The doctor of the future will no longer treat the human frame with drugs, but rather will cure and prevent disease with nutrition."
—Thomas Edison

INTRODUCTION

I love learning from philosophers throughout the ages, and the more I read the words and aphorisms of great thinkers, the more I realize how many wise conclusions seem to be the clever observation of opposites.

Take the modern-day philosophy of Dr. Evil's obese henchman of *Austin Powers* fame, who says, "I eat because I'm unhappy and I'm unhappy because I eat!"

I was in trouble a lot as a child. Most of my school reports contained words to the effect of "David is a pleasant and well-mannered young man; however, he is easily distracted and in turn can be a source of distraction to others."

I was often sent from the classroom to the principal's office for bad behavior and punished with a very long cane.

I remember one principal, soon after starting in the role, giving me a right royal hiding in front of the entire class for cracking a wise-guy joke. He threw me into the chalkboard wall, tearing my shirt from my back in the process.

At the time, I thought I deserved the punishment, but in his office he apologized profusely and replaced my torn shirt with a brand-new school shirt that matched those of every other boy in the class. I had only ever worn hand-me-downs until this day.

He made me promise that I would not tell my parents. I kept the promise, kept the shirt, and kept my distance from his office from that day on. Until one day the following week, when I got into a fight with a school bully who flushed my tie down the toilet.

Moments later, I was standing outside the principal's office, regretting my behavior.

He called me in, sat me down, and asked if I had ever watched John Wayne in a cowboys-and-Indians movie. He then told me the following story:

"There was a Cherokee tribe who would gather every Friday night to watch a wolf fight between the chief's white and black wolves. Each of the tribe members would place bets and after all the bets were cast, the chief would predict who he thought would win.

"The tribe was amazed that over five years of fights, the chief's predictions were always correct. When some of the elders asked how he got it right all the time, he replied: 'I knew which wolf would win because I knew which one I had fed all week.'"

The principal explained that I had both a black wolf and a white wolf inside me and whichever I fed would be the behavior I demonstrated. He suggested I should focus on the white wolf, which he deemed the good wolf, and try not to feed its black counterpart, which he aligned with bad temper and bad behavior.

Many years later, I recounted this story to a client. On the back of its message, she lost over 25 kilograms (55 pounds).

I asked her what name she best liked being called and she said she loved it when her husband called her "Goddess." Then I asked her the opposing question, and she told me she decided to leave her ex-husband the first and last time he ever called her a "fat cow."

To curb her bad eating habits, I asked her to consider asking herself this question whenever she went to a fridge, pantry, supermarket, café, or restaurant:

"Who am I about to feed, the Goddess or the cow?"

We all have the capacity to fuel our better self, our "white wolf."

Why It Matters

A vegan, an atheist, and a CrossFitter walked into a bar. I only know this because they told everyone within two minutes of walking in …

I work with all sorts of people across all life stages. My shredding for the wedding program rarely sees couples present with the same weight-loss goals, but that doesn't mean they can't work out or plan their meals together.

They both want to look and feel their absolute best on their wedding day, and we generally work toward the date of their final dress and suit fittings.

I also work with couples looking to have their first child. Couples who want a healthy bodily environment for the beginning, middle, and end of the greatest responsibility they will ever have: raising children. In essence, couples who want happiness and well-being.

As with exercise, the power word acrostic for happiness and well-being applies to weight loss as well:

LEANER
Less
Eating
And
Normalize
Exercise
Routines

"While overeating would be seen by some as an indulgence of self, it is in fact a profound rejection of self. It is a moment of self-betrayal and self-punishment, and anything but a commitment to one's own well-being."

—Marianna Williamson, author and politician

CHAPTER 17:

Eating Plans

"The secret to living well and longer is: eat half, walk double, laugh triple, and love without measure."
—Tibetan proverb

The *Merriam-Webster Dictionary* tells us the word diet "first appeared in English in the 13th century. Its original meaning was the same as in modern English, 'habitually taken food and drink.'"

It also tells us that "the word diet was used in another sense too in the Middle and early modern English periods to mean 'way of living.'"

But rather than use the word diet, which I believe has come to mean restriction and suffering, I prefer to say "eating plans."

As with spirituality and exercise, it's not for me to tell you which is the best eating plan for you to adopt; rather, it is to offer eating plan suggestions.

You get to choose which eating plan will give you peace of mind and be sustainable in sustaining you.

As with exercise routines, there are many plans to choose from based on your goals.

The simplest eating plan is the one told to me by my doctor: less eating.

He says it is good to feel a little bit hungry throughout the day. Being able to go lengthy periods of time without food is one of the greatest determinants of longevity.

And I believe that apart from the fact that fasting mops up the bad cells within the body to use as fuel, it also increases the power of the mind.

It builds self-discipline, too. It also ramps up self-awareness of the mind-body connection: I hunger therefore I am.

There is also a sense of self-empowerment in having stuck to your guns and not given in to temptation.

The other simple and very manageable eating plan that doesn't require complex calorie calculations and portion control is avoiding wheat, dairy, and sugar products. Do this for two weeks.

I say "simple" because you don't have to think too much about it.

If you are at a cocktail party, it's not whether you have one piece of cheese or seven—you have none, because dairy is off limits. Same with the caramel slice, because sugar is a no-no.

And at the breakfast buffet, you don't have to worry about choosing between wheat products such as toast and croissants.

As your ability to say no increases, things become easier.

It's like Saint Augustine said: "Complete abstinence is easier than perfect moderation."

Especially when it comes to alcohol consumption.

Many years ago, on my way home from the gym, I stopped off at a bakery and asked for some wheat-free, yeast-free bread. I explained to the baker that I was avoiding wheat and yeast, and he asked me whether I could drink beer and eat pizza. When I told him I couldn't, he joked: "You'd be better off dead, wouldn't you?"

His was not an uncommon attitude at the time. It was the same with beer and wine. Any time I tried to avoid alcohol I was met with derision and zero support from so-called friends.

All my clients have achieved their weight-loss and wellness goals only when they have eliminated alcohol from their system.

Once alcohol enters the bloodstream, your body attempts to rid your system of what it believes to be poison. Every other calorie burning effort is turned toward eliminating and detoxifying your body from alcohol.

I abstained from alcohol for one year as an example for my clients and as a personal social experiment. Many of my clients followed suit and all of them reached their goal weight. To this day, many still don't imbibe.

At the end of the day, any plan that you set for yourself must be realistic.

There are many diets, but some are downright ridiculous. Any breatharians out there? Short-lived on every level …

Be kind to your future self.

If we reverse-crystal ball and you have children or plan to, you should look at your children as your future self. Don't let your "kindness" be their cruelty. If you wouldn't eat a particular food, don't feed it to them.

Munchausen syndrome by proxy is a mental illness and a form of child abuse. The caretaker of a child, most often a mother, either makes up fake symptoms or causes real symptoms to make it look like the child is sick.

Now known as Factitious Disorder Imposed on Another (FDIA), it should be known as Factitiously Imposed Disorder on Another (FIDA), pronounced as "feeder," to make the "carer" realize that they are the feeder.

Parents and carers place locks on medicine cabinets and cupboards which contain cleaning chemicals and poisons yet allow their children free reign in the snacks cupboard.

"Let food be thy medicine," Hippocrates, the father of medicine, said.

People think it was easier back in Hippocrates' time (460–370 BC) to prescribe food as medicine, because there wasn't the same level of processed foods as we have today.

Yet there is evidence of beer, tortillas, wine, cheese, olives, and palm oil going back more than 7000 years.

Hippocrates lived to the ripe old age of 90, so I'm going to put my money on his philosophy rather than the slick marketing campaigns used to promote the consumption of processed foods we have foisted on us today.

Around the time I started weight-training, I struggled with a guilty secret. I wanted to have big muscles like my brother Kevin, so I started, *serially*, stealing his breakfast cereal.

His cereal of choice was Kellogg's Nutri-Grain, or "Ironman food" as it was marketed, and the advertisements showed muscular men wolfing it down and then winning Ironman races.

The "positively persuaded publisher" who started me in my $25,000-a-year dream job also paid for me to study marketing at university while I worked for him. The first night I attended, the lecturer outlined the trickeries of marketing, explaining that there was just as much sugar in the Ironman food known as Nutri-Grain as there was in Coco Pops.

When I was a kid, the Coco Pops mascot was a monkey. I felt like one when I discovered this ruse and felt another sense of guilt for stealing my brother Kevin's cereal. Aside from what is added to the processed foods we eat; we also add our own "sweet poisons."

In his book *Sweet Poison*, David Gillespie states that our primary appetite control mechanism—the hypothalamus—releases the hormones which regulate appetite.

He says that every piece of food we eat releases "enough to eat" hormones, once we have in fact, had enough to eat. That is, except for one substance: fructose. Fructose is a natural sugar found on its own in fruit, but is also one of the components of sucrose, the scientific name for table sugar.

Fructose also slips by the fat control mechanism in the liver, Gillespie points out, and it skips to the front of the queue to be converted to fatty acids and then body fat.

"We can eat as much fructose as we can shove down our throats and never feel full for long," he says. But I reckon that on its own, fructose found explicitly in fruit, juices, some vegetables, and honey is difficult to shove down your throat in vast quantities, and I think it is a terrible shame to avoid seasonal fruits such as mangoes or a ripe peach in summer as a component of an eating plan.

The health department's recommendation of five vegetables and two pieces of fruit a day is fair in this regard. I recommend that these two pieces of fruit be the only "sugar" you let into the temple door. The temple being your body.

Avoid juices in vast quantities in your initial weight-loss campaign, as you are better off with the fiber content of pieces of fruit for overall digestion and vitamin retention. Once you are at your fighting weight, juices can be used as detoxifiers, cleansers, and energizers.

My personal sweetest poison is chocolate. Dark chocolate, however, is difficult to shove down your throat at any cocoa level above 70 percent. It is a great antioxidant.

It is the sugar added to cocoa which makes milk chocolate so moreish. A challenge I give to my clients is to avoid milk chocolate for 40 days—and it's not as hard as you think. Unlike alcohol, for example, there are no chocolate clubs, or venues where people gather as a cohort to chomp down on Mars Bars. Just keep it out of the house for 40 days.

But don't offload your unwanted chocolate to friends. If you wouldn't eat it, don't poison your friends with it. It is no shame to waste manufactured foods; it is a great shame to waste natural foods.

Xocolatophobia is the fear of chocolate. You must become xocolatophobic.

I tell clients to go to bed early so they can hide from themselves. And in the case of chocolate lovers, so that they can hide from chocolate. Chocolate also contains caffeine, so the "hits" keep coming. I have a rule for myself: when I mindfully choose to eat chocolate, I allow a reasonable amount and stand up and look out the window while I do. This avoids discovering the chocolate is all gone as I mindlessly consume it.

Some people even hit the sack early to avoid alcohol and the accompanying cigarettes they would have if they were drinking. Personally, I brush my teeth as soon as I have planned to stop eating of an evening, which I think sends signals to the brain from my childhood habits that all eating is done for the day, so I should ready myself for bed.

I met famous British chef Heston Blumenthal at the launch of a food processor many years ago and he told me salt was one of his favorite things to cook with.

Adding salt to meals at the table is linked to an earlier death, according to a Biobank study of 500,000 middle-aged Britons.

Researchers found that always adding salt to food knocks more than two years off the life expectancy of men and one-and-a-half years off women, not including seasoning during the cooking process. A doctor would recommend that the best way to lower blood pressure would be by consuming less salt.

Compared with those who never or rarely added salt, those regular salt seasoners had a 28 percent increased risk of dying prematurely. At the age of 50, men and women who always added salt had a life expectancy 2.3 years and 1.5 years shorter respectively.

To counterbalance salt intake, it was recommended salt lovers adopt a diet rich in fruit and vegetables. Those with an elevated risk of heart disease were warned to cut down.

Of course, less sugar and salt should be a simple part of your overall eating plan. As with exercise, I don't recommend short-term fixes or intense diets, because I have witnessed the yo-yo effect these approaches can have.

However, two extreme weight-loss choices do work: the ketogenic diet and quitting alcohol.

I met Mark Sisson, primal movement guru and author of *Ketosis Reset Diet*, in 2015.

Mark writes: "Ketosis suppresses appetite, which may be the most important feature of the keto diet. The overriding drive to eat more food is the biggest impediment to weight loss, and it's the reason why most diets fail. When people attempt to eat less food despite wanting more, they butt up against their own physiology. Few win that battle."

Ketogenic dieting avoids this issue altogether, suppressing the increase in hunger hormones that normally occurs after weight loss.

Ketogenic diets are especially effective in achieving massive weight loss. Ketosis can help you lose body fat. Again, not because of any inherent fat-burning quality of the ketones, but because in making ketones you have to liberate stored body fat.

The ketogenic diet is essentially the removal of all carbohydrates from your diet (or less than 30 grams of carbs a day) and the consumption of higher amounts of fats and protein. The ketogenic diet kicks off your day with a Bulletproof coffee. Black coffee with butter in it.

I like to provide clients with their daily macronutrient requirements (carbs, fats, protein) along with the total number of calories they should consume based on their goals and total daily energy expenditure.

I then give them a list of the high-quality food groups they can get their macros from, and I highlight superfoods.

The superfoods are:

- **Avocado** is high in fiber, reduces inflammation, and is a great source of potassium, which helps to regulate nerve function. It's high in monounsaturated fats, which lowers LDL (lousy) the bad cholesterol and supports HDL (healthy) the good cholesterol. Too much LDL cholesterol hardens and narrows your arteries, which reduces blood flow and can cause blood clots.

- **Eggs** are my go-to food and contain all the essential amino acids and vitamins we need except for vitamin C, which is why they are often served with orange juice at breakfast. I recommend boiling them to add to the feeling-full factor.

- **Salmon** is packed full of nutrients and healthy fats and is a great source of protein, B vitamins, potassium, and selenium. Salmon also provides omega-3 fatty acids, which help prevent heart disease.

- **Mushrooms** are low in calories and are a great source of fiber and protein. I've seen advertisements that call them "meat for vegetarians." Mushrooms contain an amino acid called ergothioneine, which research has shown slows down cognitive decline. Their antioxidant and anti-inflammatory compounds also protect the body from oxidative stress and disease.

- **Olive oil** is rich in antioxidants such as vitamins E and K, which protect against cellular damage from oxidative stress. Several large studies demonstrate that people who consume olive oil have a much lower risk of stroke, the second biggest killer in developed countries. Olive oil contains many nutrients that inhibit or destroy the harmful bacteria *helicobacter pylori*, which can live in the gut and cause stomach cancer.

By combining one serving of all of the above, you have a protein-rich breakfast and a great 700 calories to fuel your morning and you, well into the day.

- **Blueberries** are rich in antioxidants, which reduce the risk of heart disease and cancer. Remember that frozen blueberries are always in season and cheaper than fresh blueberries. Freezing them disrupts the cell structures, which makes it easier for our digestive system to access the rich antioxidants housed in their skins.

- **Oats** were a staple for me as a child during the winter months, and it was my job to stir the big pot of porridge that fed my nine siblings. Part of my evening ritual now is preparing for tomorrow, so I soak oats, chia seeds, milk, and yogurt overnight, known as overnight oats or Bircher muesli. Oats are high in beta-glucan, a fiber that lowers LDL (bad) cholesterol, in turn reducing the risk of heart disease.

- **Bananas** are a great pre- or post-workout inclusion and are loaded with potassium, which is vital for healthy kidneys and regulating blood pressure. They are high in easily digested carbs and magnesium. Potassium and magnesium act like electrolytes, making the banana nature's Gatorade.
- **Cinnamon** is excellent as a sugar substitute. Interestingly, studies show that adding cinnamon to drinks or foods results in lowered insulin levels and increases insulin sensitivity, which assists in the management of diabetes.
- **Yogurt** is high in protein, calcium, vitamins, and probiotics, which improve gut microbiota and, in turn, the immune system. A whopping 70 percent of your immune system is located in the gut.
- **Nuts** are my snack food of choice. They are rich in protein, and most nuts have very similar macronutrient profiles. They're full of monounsaturated fats and low in saturated fats. They also contain the amino acid arginine, which maintains blood vessel health. Individual serving sizes for nuts should be: 30 almonds, 10 Brazil nuts, 15 cashews, 20 hazelnuts, 15 macadamias, 15 pecans, 30 pistachios, 10 whole walnuts, and a small handful of peanuts or mixed nuts.
- **Ginger** is the best-tasting antibacterial. It halts the growth of the *E. coli* stomach bug, which creates diarrhea. Compounds within ginger called gingerols are considered to be anticancer and high in antioxidants.
- **Garlic** is a natural antibiotic which many people avoid because of its smell. Allicin is its active ingredient and contains the sulphur-rich compound which makes garlic a superfood. Whenever I feel as though I'm getting sick, I put two whole cloves of garlic into a beetroot, carrot, celery, ginger, and apple juice extraction and down it immediately.
- **Sweet potato** is relatively low in sugar, packed with potassium, and a good source of fiber and vitamins C and A.
- **Dark leafy greens.** Popeye was bang on when he said: "I am what I am and that's all that I am." Several studies link the consumption of spinach to the prevention of prostate and breast cancer. It's also high in antioxidants.
- **Beetroot** is my favorite vegetable. It supports heart, brain, and digestive health. It is brilliant as a pre-workout juice because it increases energy production and enhances blood flow to muscles.
- **Turmeric's** active ingredient is curcumin, which is a powerful antioxidant, anti-inflammatory, and anti-fungal. It eases arthritis symptoms, and studies

have shown that it may protect the aging brain. Some studies have shown turmeric to be beneficial in the treatment of Parkinson's disease.

All the above foods combine well to form breakfast, lunch, or dinner meals.

Steak is my absolute favorite food but, alas, it isn't necessarily considered a superfood by anyone other than the proponents of the carnivore diet …

"How do I like my steak? Right next to my other steak."
—Larry Riley

CHAPTER 18:

Meal Methods

═══════════

"Reminds me of my safari in Africa. Somebody forgot
the corkscrew and for several days we had to live on nothing
but food and water."
—W.C. Fields

Some of my clients who follow a macros-specific eating plan are initially shocked by how high the carbohydrate component is. They don't realize that carbohydrates provide the energy for their overall training and exercise campaign.

Over the years, carbohydrates have been demonized. I know people who avoid carbs all week and then drink their weekly carb intake in white wine on a Friday night.

While drinking my carbs of a weekend wasn't my philosophy, I used to abstain from alcohol on weekdays. Many years ago, a doctor advised me that I should have two AFDs a week.

"What are AFDs?" I asked.

"Alcohol-Free Days."

She told me that the liver needs a break to recover and do its real job, which is to process the blood leaving the stomach, creating nutrients through metabolizing fats, proteins, and carbohydrates.

She also said that AFDs help prevent alcohol-related cancers.

"I have five AFDs a week then!" I proudly exclaimed.

"Well, just make sure the other two days aren't DFAs!" she shot back.

"What's a DFA?" I asked.

"Drinking for Australia."

Crash diets that promise rapid weight loss are never sustainable. The calorie reduction figure you should be aiming for is 500 grams per week.

There are 7700 calories in 1kg (2.2lb) of fat. If you want to lose 1kg (2.2lb) of fat, you can either burn that many calories through energy output (exercise) or create a calorie deficit of 7700 through less eating.

If you have a lot of weight to lose, cutting out 1100 calories a day from your diet over seven days would see you lose 1kg (2.2lb) a week.

But if you are of average weight, not managing the foods you consume runs the risk of losing muscle mass in this process.

Your body does not store amino acids, as it does with carbohydrates and fat, which is why muscle breakdown is the only way to release amino acids for fuel. Muscle loss in older adults is known as sarcopenia, an involuntary loss of skeletal muscle mass and strength, which can start in the early 40s.

Muscle mass is a major determinant of health span, and sarcopenia is linked to many later life accidents and injuries. Strong muscles aid in balance and coordination. If you don't want to be helped out of the bath in later years, do squats and take the stairs wherever possible.

It's only when your body is in starvation mode, where all fat reserves have been depleted, that protein is used as fuel. Let's worry about that problem when we get there. Depending on the realistic end goal of your desired weight, its achievability will depend on several factors.

The single biggest factor is "why?" Why do you really want to achieve the goals you have set? Then you need to ask "what." What will your "why" give you? "What" will make your "why" happen?

During the height of COVID, my youngest daughter told me she wanted to lose 5kg (11lb). She said she wanted to be the same weight she was in high school.

I recently sent her a photo of her training in my gym during COVID and she agreed that she really did look fantastic. She still does. And she is happy.

I'm a big believer in avoiding self-comparisons. Theodore Roosevelt said: "Comparison is the thief of joy."

After I left primary school for high school, I remember being in the change rooms for our first swimming session, and a classmate pointing at me and yelling: "Lee! You're fat!"

Then everyone in the change room shouted: "Potbelly Lee," which became my nickname.

I avoided the pool for the rest of the swim season, but the incident motivated me to lose the gut. Ridicule has that effect.

I started running daily, watching what I ate, and lifting weights with my brother Kevin. The following summer, I removed my shirt at the first swimming session, and my nickname immediately changed to "Mr. Muscles" and "Rambo."

Soon afterward, I came across a quote by Ernest Hemmingway: "It's not about being better than your fellow man, it's about being better than the man you were yesterday."

The real idea is that jealous people just want to label you, so whether you are fat or fit, you will never win unless you are happy that the race is with and within yourself. Be careful of who your friends are and the "advice" they give you. I have found that it is my clients' friendship groups that are most likely to derail their life-changing plans.

They don't want to see you lift your game as it will require them to lift theirs.

Weight loss is a tough journey quite often taken alone. Anyone who knew your "old you" should applaud and acknowledge the "new you." If they do; keep them as friends. If they don't, keep your distance. Ultimately, the only person you really need to be happy with is the person in the mirror.

As my friend Larry Riley says: "Your first mistake is caring what people think and your second mistake is thinking that they care."

To begin a fitness plan, I recommend you get a DEXA scan, as a before-and-after barometer of your progress.

DEXA stands for Dual-Energy X-ray Absorptiometry and is a medical imaging test which uses very low levels of x-rays to measure your weight in muscle, fat, bone, and water.

During the six years I was with *Australian Men's Fitness* magazine, we had DEXA scans every three months as a way of measuring the effectiveness of different eating plans and exercise regimes we undertook for editorial purposes.

Every year for the past 20, I have ramped up my fitness levels campaign three months out from my next birthday, so that I would feel great for the big day.

Twelve weeks out from my most recent birthday, I booked a DEXA scan.

I asked the clinic owner if he had my results from 10 years ago, and it turned out I had lower body weight, less body fat, and more muscle weight back then. But the day I visited I hadn't ever felt stronger, fitter, or happier.

He reassured me: "Who cares what you may have looked like, or what your scans told you from 10 years ago? If you can say today that you've never been happier, isn't that what we are all after?"

On my way home, I remembered that 10 years ago, I was "hangry" most of the time and eating very boring and repetitive meals. I was also in pain from so many high-intensity workouts, and I only socialized or relaxed on Friday and Saturday nights.

Your eating plan will be different depending on whether you want to lose 5kg (11lb), 10kg (22lb), 15kg (33lb), or 20kg (45lb). Whatever the goal, you will need to change the way you look at food and the way you consume it.

For example, breakfast doesn't have to be at a set time. You are literally breaking the fast and this can be done at any time of day. And what you eat doesn't have to be dictated by tradition. A 220g eye fillet steak and eggs is one of my favorite first meals of the day, followed by a handful of nuts for additional protein and for fiber when I'm training for strength and muscle.

Using me as an example, here are some fat-loss paths you could take.

One kilogram (2.2lb) of fat equates to 7700 calories.

As a man in my mid-fifties, I have a total daily energy expenditure (TDEE) of 2550 calories. This is the number of calories my body will burn without exercise.

So, on a rest day I can eat 2550 calories a day and not put on or lose any weight.

If I want to lose 6kg (13lb) in 12 weeks (84 days) in a healthy and sustainable manner, I could do either of two things:

Adjust my eating and cut back on 550 calories a day (typically breakfast) and not exercise, which will take me two weeks (14 x 550) to lose 7700 calories or 1kg (2.2lb) of fat. 84 days x 550 = 46,200 calories reduced in total, which, divided by 7700, equals 6kg (13lb).

Or

I will not adjust my eating and commit to moving seven days a week, training until my heart rate monitor shows me I've burned 550 calories each day, which will give me the same result.

If I want to lose 6kg (13lb) in 6 weeks, I could do the following:

Cut back on 550 calories a day (typically breakfast) which will take me two weeks to lose 7700 calories or 1 kg (2.2lb) of fat, keeping this calorie restriction constant for 42 days.

Plus

Commit to moving seven days a week, where I will train until my heart rate monitor shows me that I've burned 550 calories each day.

This could comprise brisk walking for an hour two days a week, one high-intensity, full-body workout session for 45 minutes, and four weightlifting sessions for 60 minutes.

Eating less and moving more is best as I am burning stress chemicals and boosting my feel-good hormones through exercise.

Another indicator of how healthy your body is and how much weight you need to shed is BMI: body mass index. To arrive at this figure, divide your weight by the square of your height.

However, as the Heart Foundation warns, it is not a fail-safe calculation: "It's important to remember that BMI is not the most reliable measure of whether your weight is in a healthy range for your height. It's not a good overall indicator of how healthy you are, and doesn't take into account important factors like age, gender, and body composition (fat, muscle, and bone)."

People who gain weight in the abdominal region have a higher risk of developing heart problems. Belly fat is a good indicator of the fat found around your organs. This fat blocks healthy blood flow and leads to serious health issues.

My first meal of the day includes at least 20 grams of protein. The word protein comes from the Greek *protos*, meaning "of first importance." That's about three large boiled eggs.

You should have a plan around what you eat and drink, and look at food as fuel for the majority of your week.

I once asked a client on a Monday morning how her weekend was, and she answered: "Well, on Saturday night I had no plans and so …"

I stopped her there and asked: "What about your eating plan?"

She was about to tell me she had gone off the rails because she went out, had too many drinks, and eaten at McDonald's on the way home. I have heard it all before. The eating plan you decide upon needs to be flexible yet portable. By portable, I mean you should be able to shift it to a restaurant or café.

Another client, who is Italian, would get worried about upcoming dinners with his grandmother because she always loaded his plate with food, particularly pasta. So, we role-played what the dinner conversations might sound like, and came up with planned responses such as:

"I want to live as long as you, Nonna, so I'm only going to eat as much as you do."

In fact, aside from the excess pasta, most of Nonna's traditional Mediterranean diet would be quite healthy, but too much of anything is bad for you. In fact, the Mediterranean diet is followed by people living in one of the world's blue zones: Sardinia in Italy.

Blue zones are regions where people tend to live the longest on average. Apart from Sardinia, the Japanese islands of Okinawa, the Nicoya Peninsula in Costa Rica, Ikaria in Greece, and Loma Linda in California are all blue zones.

As disparate as these places are in terms of geography and culture, what they have in common is their citizens follow a predominantly plant-based diet and drink lots of green tea.

The big surprise is that a city in the United States is on the list given that the US has the highest incidence of obesity in the developed world.

A majority of the residents of Loma Linda are Seventh-day Adventists. They abstain from caffeine and avoid alcohol and most meat products. They also have a very prayerful way of living.

They see their bodies as the "temple of the Holy Spirit," and their diet is based around interpretations of the Old Testament, specifically Genesis 1:29: "Then God said, 'I give you every seed-bearing plant on the face of the whole earth and every tree that has fruit with seed in it. They will be yours for food.'"

In 2016, according to the World Health Organization, more than 1.9 billion adults worldwide were overweight. The prevalence of obesity tripled worldwide between 1975 and 2016.

I think fasting contributes to longevity, because as with any practice of self-discipline, the mind is strengthened, leading to better life decisions.

Daily fasting has been scientifically proven to play a significant role in longevity. It lowers all metabolic syndrome markers such as blood pressure, sugar levels, cholesterol, and triglycerides.

If you are considering whether your upcoming meal choice is right for you, ask yourself whether it was grown in the sun. If it wasn't (apart from mushrooms), don't eat it, or in the very least, consume the processed food sparingly.

Trash processed food. Don't wait until it is finished. Don't think you're wasting it. If the food has been processed, it has already been laid to waste.

Processed meat is a definite no-no because of its high sodium content and carcinogenic risks. Trial a meat-free Monday to get on top of your red meat consumption.

An excellent alternative to meat is fish, but you have to be aware that even the choicest tuna and salmon contain high levels of mercury. These oily fish are good for heart health, but several types of white fish are also low in fat and high in protein if you don't cook them in batter and sweet sauces.

Some people complain that steamed fish is for nursing homes and hospitals, but that's where you might end up if you don't consider healthy meal options like this. Be creative. Search the net for recipes that are easy to prep and put on the plate.

Chicken and turkey are terrific lean sources of protein, but kangaroo, which is around 98 percent fat-free protein, should be high on your shopping list. Game meats are low in fat and have a high net protein utilization (NPU).

NPU is a measure of how well your body digests and retains protein from a food source. The top five NPU foods are eggs (98 percent), fish (89 percent), chicken (85 percent), beef (82 percent), and lamb (80 percent).

Remember: fresh, healthy food is expensive but so are hospital bills and funerals.

"Develop a level of private self-righteousness. Don't tell them how you're living, let your epitaph tell them how you lived."
—Larry Riley

CHAPTER 19:

Gut Health

═══════════

"All disease begins in the gut."
–Hippocrates

The ancient Greeks knew what modern medicine is only now beginning to learn: how well your gut functions is key to how well your body and mind function.

At one stage they believed that our brains were in our gut. That our thoughts were controlled by what was in our stomach. I think they were on to something.

I also believe you are what you think, and that what and how you think is affected by what and how you eat.

You should treat your gut like a garden and feed it with nutrients and water for growth and survival. Think of your gut as your "**g**arden **u**nder **t**hreat." Processed foods and drinks are thistles and weeds. Your gut has one gardener. You.

Can you agree that what you eat and drink may be contributing to how you think and feel?

Seventy percent of your immune system is located in your gut. There is now a field of psychology known as gut-brain psychology. Science has established there are neurons in the gut with similar nerve chemicals to those found in the brain. They refer to this as the enteric brain. Your gut brain.

Ninety percent of serotonin, your feel-good hormone, is produced within your gut.

Eighty percent of the vagus nerve sends signals to the brain from the gut.

The brain and the brain stem are where the vagus nerve begins its route. Within the brain, this nerve regulates anxiety and depression. It is responsible for processing, digesting, and moving what you eat and drink freely along the digestive system. When the vagus nerve is damaged, the entire digestive system is thrown off-kilter.

Retraining the nerve can be done by gargling water several times a day for a few weeks and binning the bad eating habits.

"Hangxiety," as I like to call it, is where you have literally killed or poisoned the good bacteria in your gut, known as *microbiota* (Greek for "small life"), through excessive alcohol intake.

The occasional glass of red wine is said to be healthy because it contains resveratrol, which is rich in antioxidants. Resveratrol may help to protect the lining of blood vessels in the heart. But a bottle of red wine will cause inflammation in your gut, which can damage the wall of the lining, leading to leaky gut syndrome. Food particles and other toxins cross the lining of your gut and enter your bloodstream, triggering negative immune responses.

If the alcohol doesn't wipe some of your good gut bacteria out, then the six cups of coffee or two cans of Red Bull the next day will.

Drink excessively often enough, and you are developing a case of "swallowing the spider to catch the fly and wondering why you swallowed the fly." And you will spend the latter part of the day tired and emotional. Curiously, the medication used to treat anxiety and depression is effective through working on your serotonin levels, which should be produced from your healthy gut.

Prebiotics and probiotics are the two great fertilizers you need to have in your garden under threat. Prebiotics are the diverse types of fiber that feed the good bacteria in the digestive system. Probiotics are beneficial bacteria found in certain foods or purchased in supplements.

Alcohol is like spraying your garden with weed killer.

Your garden bed needs to be solid enough to keep the nutrients in. One of my favorite gut healers is also exceptionally low in calories and easy to make and store. Bone broth contains the amino acid glycine which will decrease inflammation and improve digestion. It's also a great pick-me-up.

It is nature's Botox. The collagen in bone broth is great for your hair, skin, teeth, and nails.

During my lifetime, I've had two knee operations. That's why I took the supplement glucosamine, which is good for joints and connective tissue. I don't take glucosamine anymore and haven't for the past 10 years because bone broth contains both glucosamine and chondroitin, which strengthens cartilage and joints.

Drinking bone broth before meals provides you with proteins that help control blood sugar levels. It's also excellent for relaxing, because it contains glycine, which calms the nervous system and enhances a positive mood. Sometimes, all I have for dinner is a cup of bone broth.

Many countries and cultures (no pun intended) have traditional foods that naturally contain probiotics. And the good news is the likes of sauerkraut, kimchi, kefir, and Greek yogurt can all be made at home.

Fiber intake is another healthy determinant of gut health. It is the intestinal rake. It helps the body remove waste particles from the digestive system.

We consume either soluble or insoluble fiber sources. Soluble fiber dissolves in water and helps lower blood pressure and glucose levels. Good sources of soluble fiber are oats, nuts, apples, blueberries, and chia seeds (there's your overnight oats doing their job), as well as beans and lentils.

Insoluble fiber doesn't dissolve in water and helps move food through your digestive system, keeping you regular and preventing constipation. Good sources include almonds, walnuts, wholegrain breads with visible seeds, quinoa, brown rice, legumes, corn, leafy greens, and fruit with edible skins such as apple and pears.

For a fiber hit, I mix leafy greens, beetroot, kale, avocado, kiwifruit, apple, and frozen pineapples in my powerful NutriBullet blender. Then I pour in fresh filtered water or coconut water and blitz it. It's a meal in a juice, loaded with all the fiber-rich skins.

My other smart prebiotic and probiotic food source is sourdough. It works well for people who don't want bread in their diet and is low in sugar and packed with nutrients. It is loaded with protein and good fiber and can improve digestion and aid immunity.

CHAPTER 20:

Hydration

═══════

"When a man slakes his thirst at the well,
he quickly turns his back on it."
—Baltasar Gracián, 17th-century Jesuit philosopher

The human body can go three weeks without food but only three days without water. This is because water works as a phenomenal multitasker in your body.

It makes up 60 percent of a person's body weight. It has many functions, including moistening mucous membranes, forming saliva to aid in digestion, lubricating the spinal cord and joints, and regulating body temperature.

The primary nutrient you need to consume when you wake up is water.

This is how I get my fill. I add the juice of one lemon and a pinch of Himalayan rock salt to 750ml (25oz) of water and then drink it through a metal straw. The acidity of the lemon juice can remove your teeth's enamel, hence the straw, but it also helps dissolve uric acid in your joints and reduce inflammation.

A lemon has 139 percent of your daily Vitamin C requirements, boosting immunity straight off the bat. The combination of lemon and salt reduces toxicity by eliminating waste from your cells.

And Himalayan rock salt is a real winner. It aids with absorption and has 84 trace minerals and electrolytes that aren't in regular table salt.

While one of the roles of water is to help balance the pH levels or acidity of your body, the lemon juice and Himalayan rock salt have an alkalizing effect.

Rather than drinking eight glasses of water a day, a better rule of thumb is 30ml (1oz) of water for every kilogram (2.2lb) of body weight.

That means a 100kg (220lb) person will require 3 liters (0.8 gallons) of water and a 60kg (130lb) person will need 1.8 liters (0.5 gallons).

If you don't get enough water into you, your vitality will suffer. A mere 5 percent dehydration will lead to a 10 to 20 percent loss in focus and strength.

There is more water in lean muscle than there is in fatty tissue. Only 40 percent of fatty tissue mass comprises water, compared to 75 percent of muscle mass.

Your first sign of dehydration is usually thirst. A headache is another. I think headaches are more relieved by the glass of water consumed with the painkillers than the actual painkillers. It should take paracetamol 30 minutes to start to neutralize pain, but it usually doesn't take that long because you are rehydrated by the water.

You won't find any painkillers in the jungle because the *parrots-eat-em-all* ...

Once again, your aim should be to have light-colored or clear urine.

Avoid alcohol where you can. Its dehydrating effects are where most of the hangover sits. Each time you urinate when drinking booze, you urinate more than you drank.

"Man is more miserable, more restless and unsatisfied than ever before, simply because half his nature, the spiritual, is starving for true food, and the other half, the material, is fed with bad food."
—Paul Brunton, 20th-century spiritual book author

CONCLUSION

*"To be always intending to make a new and better life but never
to find time to set about it, is as to put off eating and drinking and
sleeping from one day to the next, until you're dead."*
—Og Mandino, author of *The Greatest Salesman in The World*

My earliest memories of food and eating were far from pleasant.

I can still remember kneeling down and praying to God as a child that I could remain alive without the need to eat. It wasn't that my mother was a bad cook, it was just that the ingredients she was cooking with weren't necessarily the best ones from which to expect a gourmet meal.

The main staples were toast or porridge for breakfast, white bread sandwiches with ox tongue and beetroot for lunch, and mashed potatoes with grilled sausages and peas for dinner. Friday night was never anything but fish, which, given we lived a long way from the sea, I abhorred. Occasional Brussels sprouts and cauliflower were a bonus if the word "bonus" meant "the worst food in the world."

Because we had such a big family, our sandwiches were made in bulk and frozen. But where I grew up, the winters were so cold that my sandwiches had quite often not defrosted by lunchtime. Frozen ox tongue, however, doesn't taste as bad as thawed ox tongue.

There were 12 of us sitting at two tables at dinner every night and my seat was the piano chair, which had no back. No one really wanted to sit in it, so I claimed it as my own, because I had a plan.

The piano chair had a lid for storing sheet music. It also doubled—with a sleight of hand and a mini air squat—as a short-term storage unit for the brussels sprouts, cauliflower, burned sausage, and fish I couldn't stand.

After dinner and before bed, I would go to the piano chair, fish out the undesirable dinner scraps, and throw them over the fence to our neighbor's dog, who wasn't as picky as I was.

The piano was only ever played by my eldest sister Patricia and my mother.

But, not being as disciplined back then as I am now, I once forgot to clean it out and my mother discovered the leftovers when she was offered money for our sheet music. My father certainly had the sheets and was not impressed once my mother told him of my musical chair affair.

The prayer of never being able to eat again but still survive is one that I am happy to say was not answered for me.

I love quality food. I love cooking and the social ritual around mealtimes, how people come together in conversation and laughter.

I love cooking for others. I love the preparation phase and imagining what guests would like to eat. I love the feedback I get during the meal and then reflecting on what we've chatted about while cleaning up after the guests have left.

I've said before that I rate the Mediterranean diet the healthiest because of its nutritional value, but I also think it is good for mental health. People from the blue zone region of Sardinia eat as a family and view meals as a wonderful time to socialize. It is a way of sharing their daily lives.

Of course, for a while now, the big gourmet trend has been toward nose-to-tail cooking, and many of the offcuts my mum served us as kids are now very fashionable in the hippest of restaurants.

Just before I turned 30, I was entertaining an important client at one of Sydney's finest dining venues, 42 levels above the city. I remember looking out at the skyline and thinking about the closing scene from the movie *White Heat* when James Cagney shouts: "Made it, Ma! Top of the world!" I texted my mother a photo of the view.

My main meal arrived at around the same time and as I started on the succulent roast lamb, I had a weird sense of taste *déjà vu*. I quietly called the waiter over and asked to see the menu again.

It confirmed what my taste buds had been trying to tell me.

"Roast Lamb with Salsa Verde and lamb tongue shavings …"

It is a fact I can attest to, that if you've tasted one tongue, you've tasted them all …

*"In a hospital, half of the patients get better
food than at home."*
—Gerhard Kocher

EXERCISE

"If real is what you can feel, smell, taste and see, then 'real' is simply electrical signals interpreted by your brain."
—Morpheus, *The Matrix*

Another benefit of fasting is that it enables you to avoid bad food. There are certain times in life—usually parties—when it seems like it's not possible to eat the way you'd like. If you're at a function and all that's on offer is pizza, remember that the human body can survive three weeks without food.

I would rather not eat than consume bad food that negatively impacts my nutrition. It is the removal of processed foods from your food intake that makes any eating plan successful. Processed foods aren't on the menu of any serious eating plan.

With your eating plan in mind, consider the following:

1. Who are you about to feed? Your white wolf or your black wolf (who may end up being the black dog of depression, because you are feeding who you don't want to be, and that will make you feel bad)?
2. Ask yourself before putting food in your mouth: "Is what I am about to eat moving me toward or away from my health and wellness goals?"
3. Ask yourself: "Is what I am about to eat the best use of my macros?" Are all your daily 50 grams of carbohydrates from one small chocolate and zero fiber?
4. Drink 30ml (1oz) of water for every kilogram (2.2lb) of your body weight, and buy a two-liter water bottle.
5. If you wouldn't eat a particular food or feed it to a sick person, don't feed it to your children. Remove all processed, packaged foods from the pantry.
6. If you'd like to start fasting, fast for 12 hours, then work up to 16 hours before you have your first meal of the day.
7. Cut back on salt.
8. Reduce alcohol intake.

"Came from a plant, eat it; was made in a plant, don't."
—Michael Pollan

5: Engagement
The Daily Pursuit of Human Connection

*"If you talk to a man in a language he understands,
that goes to his head. If you talk to him in his language,
that goes to his heart."*
—Nelson Mandela

INTRODUCTION

When my daughters were about to start school, I moved interstate for a two-year contract and joined the local aquatic center, which also had a gym and a sauna.

The sauna was frequented by men with thick accents from all around the world.

I remember an Italian man saying hello to me by name, but I couldn't remember his. I asked my new best friend George, who was Greek, what the fellow's name was.

"Guess," he answered, rubbing his stomach, as he always did.

"Mario?" I offered.

"No. Guess, guess," he kept on.

I started rattling off the names of any Italian man I had ever met. "Giuseppe, Dino, Roberto …"

George was confused. In his heavy Greek accent, he cried: "Stop! Who are these people? Guess! His name is Guess! Au-guess-tus."

Gus. Augustus. Of course!

And as Augustus, first emperor of Rome said: "Young men, listen to an old man to whom old men listened when he was young."

Before my daughters began school, we only had one swing in our backyard.

I would push each daughter on the swing and sing "Moonshadow," a song by Cat Stephens which went for three minutes, the perfect amount of time for a good push.

A neighbor heard me singing it and asked whose song it was. When I told him it was Cat Stevens, he said, "He sings 'Cat's in the Cradle,' doesn't he?"

But that's a Harry Chapin tune, and to prove it, I played the song loudly on our sound system.

Hearing it for the first time, my youngest daughter asked me what the words meant.

Basically, it tells the story of a father who is so busy he misses all the milestones in his son's life. And when the boy becomes a man, he repeats the sins of the father and has no time for his dad.

From that day on, she would start singing the song under her breath—but just loud enough for me to hear—whenever I told her I was too busy to spend time with her.

It had the desired effect. I would drop whatever I was doing and give her my time. And I'm so glad I did. I have never regretted a single moment I spent with my daughters.

Parents who have poor relationships with their children are often annoyed by their behavior. But in many cases, kids are just replicating what they have seen their parents do.

I often hear: "When I ask my son how school was today, he answers with an inaudible grunt."

That's because he will have noticed that the parent didn't really want more than a one-word answer, that the parent was too busy scrolling through their phone or working on their laptop. The parent was not present, not engaged. Is it any wonder he responded so indifferently?

Why It Matters

When I was in my later years at high school, permission was granted for students to smoke in the schoolyard if they had a note from a parent. Progressive at the time, regressive today.

I wasn't a smoker, but I wanted to fit in, so I forged my brother Anthony's signature, claiming he was my guardian.

Then I asked schoolyard smokers for cigarettes.

I probably lost more friends begging for smokes than I gained anyway.

I didn't like the habit. I didn't like the taste or smell, and it gave me a terrible headache.

Being able to hand-roll tobacco was seen as the height of cool.

One day as I was trying to roll a cigarette, I noticed that written under the top flap of the pouch of this particular brand of tobacco was the phrase: "A friend is another, just like you."

Quality friendships play a key role in our mental and physical well-being.

I saw an older gentleman I knew out for a walk one day and I asked him how he was.

"Oh, I can't complain," he said. "Apart from that, I'm not too bad." He is a smart man.

Use it or lose it applies to friends as well. You must flex your social muscles as often as possible. Engage with friends, and even strangers, at every opportunity, because you never know how many opportunities you have left, and a simple "How are you doing?" has the potential to change someone's day.

The concept of paying it forward, as in buying the stranger behind you a coffee, is well-known, but paying it forward with kindness can mean so much more to someone than just a free caffeine hit.

Friends with benefits means that friends benefit from the social connection with you. Many a get-well card has gotten many a person well.

> *"Some people bring joy wherever they go,*
> *others whenever they go."*
> —Oscar Wilde

CHAPTER 21:

Family

═══════════

"Think of your family today and every day thereafter; don't let the busy world of today keep you from showing how much you love and appreciate your family."
—Josiah, 648–809 BC

The above quote is taken from the Old Testament and attributed to the King of Judah.

Apart from warring, his "busy" world would have seen him travel as far as a camel or a donkey could take him.

He only lived to the age of 39, so some might think that he died early from an indulgent king's lifestyle, but he was fatally wounded by Egyptian archers.

Around this time, the Great Pyramid of Giza was completed. If the king decided to take a trip by camel to see it for a family holiday (King Josiah had four sons), it would have taken him around six days.

If he decided to go there on a business trip to do some trading, he would have been gone for almost two weeks, so he had a point when he said family are everything.

How many days collectively do you spend away from your family or partner on business?

Consider your interstate or international business trips and add on the overtime you put in over your eight hours of contracted work every day.

Some people spend as much as 12 weeks away from their family each year in unpaid overtime.

I was at a "Father's Friday" event at my children's school, and one of the dads was on the phone doing business, pacing up and down outside the classroom while his daughter was sitting alone in the classroom, watching all the other dads engaging with their children.

Noticing what was going on, I suggested he might have been better off keeping his daughter home from school to save her the embarrassment she was experiencing through his "presence of absence." He responded in a half-joking manner that he had to pay her school fees.

Phantom limb syndrome is when an amputee can still feel the sensation of their missing limb.

I hear of people thinking they can feel their phone is vibrating when it's not.

I have a rule with easily distracted clients that phones must be switched off, especially when I am addressing addictions and time management.

Allowing an engagement to be interrupted to answer a ringing phone disengages you from your immediate present.

This is an important question: Out of family, money, and health, which is your top priority?

A lot of people say family, but young people often pick money.

The wisest people will choose health.

I have a client who was told by her siblings as a child that she was adopted. They told her not to bother asking her parents whether it was true because the parents would deny it on account of feeling sorry for her. That client is now the most successful person in her family because she tried so hard to be a part of that family from an early age.

I know women who are incredibly successful from a career and financial perspective, who would give it all away because they are now past childbearing age and regret not having kids.

"Family First" is a good motto to have when it comes to a work-life balance.

People treat you the way you allow them to, so if you have family, you should communicate up front to your employer that they are your number-one priority.

Within most employment contracts, there is a clause that states from time to time you will be expected to work extra hours. But no employment contract is set in stone. You can change it to suit your family's needs. Add in: "From time to time I may be called away to family events which will be unavoidable."

My father worked very hard, but not late, and he was always home for dinner. But he wasn't present at many school events, sporting or otherwise.

On the odd occasion he came to one, I would magically win all my races or score a goal, such is the power of parental support.

On a weekend, he would take us to church and the local Olympic pool, which opened seasonally from spring to autumn. The water was always freezing, and I spent as little time as possible in it. We would also walk with him to a park far away from our home to play cricket, known only to us as "the faraway park."

But I still feel as though I missed out on some great experiences with my father, so I made sure I was there at every event my children had during their schooling years.

I chose jobs according to the flexibility they offered, so that I could work my calendar and meetings around the things that were important to my family.

At work functions, I mastered the art of shaking the hands of the host and my VIP clients and making sure they were happy so that I could leave in time for my daughter's dance or singing performance.

Rituals are important memory and meaning builders. What some may see as routines, I see as rituals.

Mealtime is a good way for a family to share their experiences from the day. If we had one of the children's friends visit for dinner, it was surprising how often they said they didn't eat together as a family.

Even if you attempt the ritual for as long as it lasts, it will be a lasting memory, good, bad, or otherwise.

I've mentioned that I think the campfire was the original television. But as sleep-inducing as a live fire can be, it is not as mind-numbing and distracting as television. Beware of it destroying your family rituals.

Depending on when you were born, you will remember the assassination of JFK, the death of Princess Diana, the shock, fear, and horror of 9/11, or the passing of Queen Elizabeth II.

You will recall vividly the time of day, the weather and deep conversations you had. That is because a memory is strengthened and embedded when there is more emotion involved. Emotion, it is said, is energy in motion. The more mundane and lackluster an experience, the less likely you are to recall it.

I remember reading *The Cat in the Hat* to my daughter one night after a particularly stressful day at work. I was reading and worrying about how I was going to solve the problems from the day. My daughter turned the page back after I had read it, and asked: "Where did you go, Daddy? I can see that you are not here." She was four at the time, but she taught me a very valuable lesson.

Creating memories is akin to creating gifts for your family and your future self.

"Wherever you go, there you are" is an expression I use to explain to people that going away on holidays isn't a guarantee they'll return refreshed and revived. Our worries and anxieties travel with us unless we change who we are and how we deal with our mindset.

If you meet a jerk in the morning, then you met a jerk. If you're meeting jerks all day every day, then you may be a jerk.

People may rob you of your money and you may waste it on things you don't need, but you can always make that money back. However, you can never get back stolen or wasted time.

I once asked a client if she only had three percent battery time left on her mobile phone and had to pick up her daughter from a location she was going to disclose in a text message, and she received a TikTok alert, would she download the TikTok?

Where are the TikToks, reels, messengers, texts, TV shows, hungover sleep-ins, business meetings, weekends away with "da boys," or "bubbles with the girls" in your life? Are they sucking up valuable bandwidth and battery life that is detracting from you creating meaningful experiences?

No one writes lengthy accounts in their journals of what happened in any of this bandwidth-stealing time and if they do, the entries are probably along the lines of "Scrolled through TikTok like a 'bingo brains' until 2:00 a.m. AGAIN last night … I promise I'll never do that again…"

I have been keeping journals for over 25 years and at the beginning of each one I write my top 10 goals for the year.

The same daughter who as a four-year-old called me out for not being present while reading *The Cat in the Hat* wrote this in the front of my journal when she was 10: "Do what you say you are going to do."

These were not words of encouragement, but the words of a child who felt I hadn't been keeping promises to her.

These days I call my schedule my *"Saidyouwill."*

I was once a guest speaker at a weekend retreat for fathers. The speaker before me had asked each of the dads to write down what they wanted their children to say about them at their funeral.

I then asked how many believed their children would be able to say these positive things about them if they had their funerals today.

I played the Johnny Cash version of "Cat's in The Cradle," and quite unexpectedly many of the men in the room cried.

Family knows and family remembers.

"A family is a place where minds come in contact with one another."
—The Buddha

CHAPTER 22:

Quality Time

═══════

*"One of the greatest gifts you can give to anyone
is the gift of attention."*
–Jim Rohn, American entrepreneur

Many men I have worked with have had bad relationships with their families. They are hard workers who spend their leisure time in solitary pursuits.

But it doesn't have to be like that. A weekly date night can help repair and rejuvenate relationships with spouses. As can a shared afternoon hobby with children.

A busy and stressed-out CEO client once told me he wanted to spend one hour of quality time a week with his children and one date night a month with his wife.

I explained to him that most divorced parents spend more time with their children than he was intending to do.

Scott Pape in his financial advice book *The Barefoot Investor* writes:

"You and your partner (or a friend) are going to get dressed up, go out to dinner, and put in place the Barefoot Steps—actually do them: set up the accounts, have the conversations while you munch on garlic bread, and have a glass of wine.

And you don't even have to do it at a restaurant. It could be a coffee shop or your bedroom, though it's much more fun to make a date of it. The important thing is that you intentionally carve out time every month to track your progress and keep yourself accountable as you follow the Barefoot Steps."

Pape is talking about financial conversations, which nobody likes to have, so I think once a month is about right.

On your date night, which I think should be at least once a week, talk about anything and everything, including money, and have an inventory-based conversation around your lifestyle together.

Author Gary Chapman says that the five love languages are words of affirmation, quality time, physical touch, acts of service, and receiving gifts.

The 5 Love Languages includes a quiz you can do to find out what your partner's love language is.

I say: "Assume your partner's love languages is *all of them*!"

Right now, by giving your partner a massage and checking in whilst at it, you are ticking each of the five love language boxes, unless you charge them $80 for the experience …

When you were dating, you would have told your partner how much you loved them and often. You probably used pet names like "Schmoopy," "Babe," or "Big Guy."

You would have cancelled on "da boys" or been unavailable for girls' nights out so that you could spend quality time with them.

You held hands in public and gave each other massages in private. You cooked their favorite meal or took them to your favorite restaurant. You spontaneously bought them gifts.

I ask people whose relationship has gone stale: When was the last time you did any of those things?

The answer is usually never within the past six months.

If you treat any relationship at the end like you did at the beginning, there would be no end to the relationship.

A friend of mine has a unique recipe for chicken schnitzel. If he left any of the ingredients out, it certainly wouldn't be his signature dish, that's for sure.

The recipe for a loving, enduring relationship will also fail if vital ingredients are left out. We use all the right ingredients during the courting phase, but later on we become complacent and feel those key elements are no longer needed. But they are. Unless you want a perpetually half-baked relationship.

"When a man spends his time giving his wife criticism and advice instead of compliments, he forgets that it was not his good judgment, but his charming manners, that won her heart."
—Helen Rowland, American journalist

CHAPTER 23:

Social

---

*"Give me a child until he is seven
and I will show you the man."*
—Aristotle

The day after my first daughter was born, the obstetrician came to check on her and told me with considerable pride that he had examined over 35,000 babies in his time and she was perfect.

"What wise advice would you give to the father of his first child?" I asked him.

"Ignore what you reward and reward what you ignore," he responded.

It wasn't until a few years later that his words made complete sense when my daughter was throwing a tantrum in the confectionary aisle of a supermarket.

As her outburst started, I kept on walking toward the checkout. Realizing she wasn't going to receive the candy she wanted, she ran after me, and clutched my hand. I picked her up and gave her a great big squeeze hug. Her tantrum was over.

I say "great big squeeze hug" because I am a serious hugger. When my children first started hugging me, I had to teach them that hugging was not something you do lightly.

I even wrote in a poem to one of my daughters: "You're so optimistic, your glass is a jug, I love how you give me a great big squeeze hug."

Hugging has been shown to increase social bonding through the release of the hormone oxytocin. Oxytocin is in fact the love hormone. Having elevated levels of it in your system is linked to feeling calmer and being able to deal better with stress.

Physical contact through hugs, massage, being intimate, shaking hands, and breast-feeding all cause the release of oxytocin.

Even the giving or receiving of a gift, or participation in a meaningful conversation, can bring it on.

As can the mere anticipation of social contact.

Oxytocin also stimulates a positive feedback loop in that it encourages us to want to socialize, which makes us feel good so that we continue to seek out relationships.

The effects of oxytocin are basically the opposite of the "fight-or-flight" response.

But make sure you hug for at least 20 seconds, because that's how you will get the biggest oxytocin hit.

Famous American psychotherapist Virginia Satir was a huge believer in the therapeutic value of hugging: "We need four hugs a day for survival. We need eight hugs a day for maintenance. We need 12 hugs a day for growth."

Echolalia is when a child repeats the words of their parents as they are learning to speak.

I still pronounce the silent "r" in many words because that's the way my Irish father spoke. On the golf course, mates would pay me out for calling a club the "nine iron."

Echopraxia is the involuntary mirroring of an observed action, like when children host tea parties and mimic the way their parents socialize.

Echophenomena is when echopraxia becomes a considered behavioral action. For example, when a young boy observes the violent behavior of his father and copies it in later life to try to resolve issues.

Monkey see, monkey do.

In 1961, Polish psychologist Albert Bandura conducted a study in Canada where children were exposed to aggressive adult behavior inflicted upon a blow-up clown doll named Bobo.

Researchers physically and verbally abused Bobo as the children looked on.

When the children were left unsupervised with the clown, they also verbally and physically abused him.

And Bobo didn't look like the scary clown from Stephen King's *It*. He had a big dopey smile.

In a follow-up study conducted in 1965, Bandura found that while children were more likely to imitate aggressive behavior if the adult model was rewarded for his or her actions, they were far less likely to imitate aggressive behavior if they saw the adult model being punished or reprimanded for their hostile behavior.

Bandura's theory was that humans tend to learn through observation, imitation, memory, and the modeling of others.

How many of your social skills have you learned through observation? How many schoolyard bullies are imitating home life? How do we correct our behaviors in new relationships when bad behaviors were tolerated in previous relationships?

And how many of our behavioral traits have we created through modeling behaviors of people we admire?

A role model is just that. Someone you model yourself on, based on the role they have played in your life.

My running style as a younger man was modeled on the character of Steve Austin from the 1970s TV series *The Six Million Dollar Man*. Steve was an astronaut whose body was repaired with bionic body parts that gave him superhuman qualities after a NASA test flight accident.

I copied his running style because I thought he was just so cool. And Lee Majors, the guy who played him, was married to pin-up actress Farrah Fawcett, so that made him even cooler …

When he was shown running, it was always in slow motion, so I was able to copy him precisely. But it wasn't until years later when I was using a sprint coach that I found out mimicking his running style, which wasn't textbook, had actually slowed me down.

I remember when my kids were not quite teenagers, they were watching a show called *The Suite Life of Zac and Cody* on pay TV. The dialogue seemed age-inappropriate to me, and I could see the characters were modelling disrespectful behaviors that were being replicated in our household.

I asked my eldest daughter to turn the television off and she replied with a firm "No."

I was taken aback.

"What part of no, don't you understand, the 'n' or the 'o'?" she went on.

I paused. "What part of 'go' don't you understand, the 'g' or the 'o'? Because that is it! Pay TV has to go. It's G-O-N-E, gone."

I cancelled the subscription, and we didn't have pay TV for many years.

So as much as I didn't ignore that behavior, I certainly didn't reward it.

"We are all born animals, it's up to society
to condition us into people."
—Larry Riley

CHAPTER 24:

Communication

═══════════

"Wisdom is the reward you get for a lifetime of listening when you'd preferred to talk."
—Doug Larson, newspaper columnist

often recoil internally when I see or hear someone giving advice they are clearly not taking themselves.

Overweight personal trainers dispensing health tips, chronically single women providing dating advice, disheveled men driving in banged-up cars offering financial guidance …

Then there are the glass-house families who spread gossip as they throw stones around their neighborhood.

My brother Kevin said his favorite dinner party conversation starter was: "What's the best advice you give that you don't take yourself?"

Teach your children well and lead by example. If you weren't taught well, it's never too late to learn and pass this knowledge on to the next generation. As a child, much of life seems to be a popularity contest. Popularity dictates fashion trends, musical preferences, and formative behaviors in general.

I remember seeing a meme of a group of teenagers all taking a selfie of themselves and the caption read: "So many selfies, so little concept of self."

Social skills can be learned and new friendships formed. We live at a time when many of the archaic social stigmas are forgotten and diversity is embraced, rather than ridiculed and admonished.

I once assisted a client in an unhappy employment situation by helping her write a CV, listing all her achievements and awards and the ways she had solved problems and made a difference at each of her previous jobs.

I reminded her of a quote from the motivational speaker Zig Ziglar, which I offer for personal relationships and workplace problems: "Your value doesn't decrease based on someone else's inability to see your worth."

After her first meeting with a recruiter, she was a little upset that because of her ethnicity, age, and sex, she was considered prime real estate in her field. She ticked all the boxes corporations want these days.

I reminded her that she had conquered all those so-called limitations anyway. That's why she was being interviewed by a prospective employer. Her worth had been valued.

I ask clients who present with "job imposter syndrome" whether their dad owns the company.

The answer is always no. But the bigger the company and role, the more likely it is they will question whether they actually deserve it. They have scored their dream job and they don't believe they are worthy of it.

Pinch yourself for sure. Just don't doubt yourself.

Self-love is first love. You can't really have love for others when you are devoid of love for yourself.

If you can, hand on heart, say that you are putting out the best version of yourself, then you should not have anything other than complete self-respect and self-confidence.

I tell friends and loved ones: "The best thing I can do for you is to look after myself; the best thing you can do for me is to look after yourself."

The self-esteem that stems from having your act together and believing in who you are is what makes making friends simple.

The golden rule comes from the Bible, in Matthew 7:12: "Do unto others as you would have them do unto you."

A hungry person will eat anything, and someone starved of love and friendship will put up with all sorts of negativity and gaslighting behavior to maintain relationships they would be better off without.

"The lonely one offers his hand too quickly to whomever he encounters," the great German philosopher Friedrich Nietzsche said.

My father was a very strict man. One of my daughter's friends asked her if I was strict when she was growing up and she said, "No, but he's very protective." I was pleased when she said that. My father was also very protective.

When I was a kid, we weren't allowed to have any friends outside of our siblings. We didn't go to other children's birthday parties and didn't attend school excursions.

We caught public transport everywhere and were instructed not to engage with anyone along the way. I was quite often punished for normal social behavior such as talking to other people.

But I did learn things. Because I wasn't able to partake myself, I had a complete fascination and curiosity in people and the way they interacted with each other. On public transport, I listened in on conversations while gazing out of train or bus windows, checking out in the reflections how people communicated, and in particular, how they used their body language, before I even knew body language was a thing.

Just prior to leaving home, I landed my first job as a mail boy at an insurance company.

I picked up heavy bags of mail from the General Post Office in the middle of the city, carrying them over my shoulder a few blocks like Santa Claus. Fax machines weren't even invented at this stage, and the most immediate form of telecommunications was via Telex message, which I had to deliver as soon it arrived. I have never worked as hard as I did back then.

When I finally left home at 18, I moved to the city and lived on my own. I had no real-life experiences to share with the outside world and was shy and insecure. But I listened and asked questions out of sheer curiosity.

I remember going to my first party, which a girl I was keen on had invited me to. Sadly, she left me as soon as we walked in, so I stood back like a wallflower and watched everything going on. I started drinking the free beer and observed.

Later, a guy everyone called Johnno arrived. He high-fived a bunch of friends, grabbed a beer, and began being the life of the party.

I ended up meeting Johnno at the ice bucket. He offered his hand for me to shake, and said, "G'day mate, I'm Johnno, what's your name?" I must have said my name timidly, because he mimicked me in a weak, high-pitched voice, then asked: "Why are you ashamed of your name, David?"

I laughed nervously. Then I asked him how he got to be so cool.

"You know what, mate," he said, "I'm actually pretty shy, I've just learned that if I pretend I'm not, everyone thinks I'm cool."

The next day, without much memory of the night before, I found myself in a bookstore looking for something to read on the beach that afternoon. That's when I discovered *How to Win Friends and Influence People* by Dale Carnegie.

From the book, I wrote down the following on a piece of paper which I carried around with me in my wallet"

Six Ways to Make People Like You:

1. Become genuinely interested in other people.
2. Smile.
3. Remember that a person's name is to that person the sweetest and most important sound in any language.
4. Be a good listener. Encourage others to talk about themselves.
5. Talk in terms of the other person's interests.
6. Make the other person feel important and do it sincerely.

These principles seemed quite easy for me to put into place as they involved an external view of people while I was engaging with them, rather than an internal view.

As a young man, I didn't really have any stories of my own to tell, other than those of a naughty childhood that wasn't all that naughty by real-world standards, so I couldn't contribute much to conversations.

By showing interest in other people, I made friends.

I had read somewhere that if you smile at yourself in the mirror for one minute, you can never be unhappy, so I did that, and still do every morning. The smile stays with me all day.

Just as Carnegie wrote, I noticed that whenever a newborn baby was brought home, which happened a lot in a 10-kid family, everyone would try to catch the baby's attention by calling out the baby's name repetitively, so it is no wonder our names are our original "safe word."

So how did I show interest in other people? I would ask what they did for a living and where they came from. I would find a person's "currency"—what made them tick. Someone once commented to me that 95 percent of my conversation with my parents centered around religion. It was hardly surprising. Religion was my parents' greatest passion.

People often tell me jokes, because they recognize that I like telling jokes and having a laugh. Years ago, I would interrupt them if I'd heard the joke before, but then I realized what they were trying to do. Now I hear the joke out because I can see the teller is trying to connect with me.

Be wary if you find people coming to you with gossip. It could very well be that they are telling you what your currency is.

As a young person I had low self-esteem. I felt other people were more important—especially older people—and the way I acted reflected that.

So, I took great solace in and confidence from Dale Carnegie's suggestions, and I began to "Johnno" my way through social gatherings and forge friendships with people I wanted to be friends with because I genuinely liked who they were.

As the Jordan Baker character in F. Scott Fitzgerald's *The Great Gatsby* said: "And I like large parties. They're so intimate. At small parties there isn't any privacy."

The Zoom phenomenon bought on by COVID is a spanner in the works from a socializing and communications perspective.

I started a contracting gig shortly after strict lockdowns were put in place and spent my days in back-to-back Zoom meetings, watching as the loud mouths of each company took control of meetings and dominated the screen.

They obviously hadn't heard this quote from Greek Stoic philosopher Epictetus: "We have two ears and one mouth so that we can listen twice as much as we speak."

I had clients who really didn't like having to look at themselves all day on camera. How many people decided they had traits they didn't like because of what they could see of themselves onscreen?

As Zoom smarts evolved, people learned to turn their microphones off or remove themselves from the screen altogether, which helped them become less self-conscious.

Many of the loud mouths I had noticed also turned their cameras off. Unless they could dominate, it seemed they didn't care to play. This leveled the playing field.

But we now had meetings from 9:00 a.m. to 5:00 p.m., leaving administrative work for post-work hours. Working from home had quickly transformed into living at work.

At the height of my advertising days there was a saying some of the cool kids had: "Losers have meetings, winners have lunches."

Human beings are the most sociable species on the planet, yet to socialize we must be able to forge a level of engagement.

The reason I believe "losers have meetings, winners have lunches" was their saying was that they knew some people hide at meetings and need a friendlier environment to articulate their ideas. Lunch is a much more convivial setting where you can really get to know a person.

As Aristotle said: "You can learn more about a person in an hour of play than you can in a year of conversation."

Of all our senses, the most important for effective communication and maintenance of friendships is hearing.

The song "Sounds of Silence" by Paul Simon and Art Garfunkel talks about people hearing but not really listening.

Garfunkel, introducing the song at a live performance in Harlem in June 1966, said it was about "the inability of people to communicate with each other, not particularly intentionally but especially emotionally, so what you see around you are people unable to love each other."

Certainly, unable to engage.

CHAPTER 25:

Listen

---

*"Courage is what it takes to stand up and speak;
courage is also what it takes to sit down and listen."*
—Winston Churchill

When I was a child, I sensed my father had a very short temper. Given his high-pressure job, I'm pretty sure having 10 kids around creating all manner of noise and mayhem didn't help.

I still remember quite vividly the day he stormed into the kitchen and shouted, "Silence!"

It was the first time I had heard the word, and the first time I remember him losing his temper. In the hush that followed, I quietly asked my eldest sister Patricia what it meant.

Patricia was only 12, but she gave me a definition that was wise beyond her years. "It means to be quiet and to listen, because the word 'silent' is spelled with the same letters as 'listen.'"

So, silence and listening have been interwoven into my way of communicating since I was a boy. In fact, the word "listen" is a great acrostic to use for everyday interaction.

It is how I teach the importance of listening skills.

L: Look.

Look into the eyes of the person you are speaking with and look to their body language as a guide to whether you should increase your level of inquiry or enthusiasm.

Communications experts such as English leadership author Graham Speechley estimate that 60 percent of our communications are non-verbal. "Listen with your eyes as well as your ears," he says.

I: Imagine/Intuit.

Asking imaginative and intuitive questions will put people at ease and show them you are interested in what they have to say. Ask open-ended questions that elicit more than a yes or no.

At this stage of the acrostic, I like to paraphrase quote Rudyard Kipling's poem "Six Honest Serving Men": "I have six honest serving friends, they taught me all I knew, their names are where and why and what and how and when and who."

S: Seek first to understand, then to be understood.

Stephen Covey's *The 7 Habits of Highly Effective People* suggests that next to physical survival, the greatest human need is psychological survival—to be understood, affirmed, validated, and appreciated.

I have spoken previously about the sauna as (almost literally) a melting pot for communication and interaction; where banter and wisdom are passed on and lots of listening is done.

When I moved interstate, there was only one other Australian who frequented the sauna I went to. His name was Gary, but everyone called him "Pop," I assume, because he was bald and talked about the "good old days" when prices were reasonable and politicians were noble.

One Saturday morning after returning from an overseas holiday, I entered the sauna to the enthusiastic greetings of expatriates in their various accents.

"That was sad about Pop dying," said George the Greek gastronome.

"Oh really?" I said in astonishment, but as I looked around I realized my Aussie mate Gary was missing. "What did he die of?" I asked.

"Old age, I would imagine," Pete the Portuguese painter posited.

"But Pop wasn't really that old, was he? He only seemed to be about 70 to me at the most," I said, still in a state of shock.

"No, he was 84!" said Vuong the Vietnamese veterinarian.

They were shaking their heads and tutting.

"How you not know Pop died?" asked Gus.

"I told you I was on holidays," I answered.

"In a cave?" asked Mick the Macedonian marketing manager.

"Holy Father 'Pop' John Paul the Second dies and you don't hear of it? He was a fellow countryman!" Paul the Polish plumber proclaimed.

Just as the penny dropped, in walked Gary as spritely as ever: "G'day, Dave! How was ya holiday, mate?"

As Stephen Covey wrote: "Most people do not listen with the intent to understand; they listen with the intent to reply."

T: Tame your tongue.

In kindergarten, I was a chatterbox and often asked by the teacher to put my index finger over my lips to stop me talking. People who know me well notice that when I am listening but itching to contribute to the conversation, I automatically put my finger over my lips.

I was in a café with a friend when two women we knew walked in. One of them was very talkative. She turned to me and asked me how I was going. She had caught me in an unguarded moment. I told her my father had died a couple of days earlier and was about to continue thinking out loud, but she laughed and started talking about herself as though I had said nothing.

When responding to a text message and you see three flickering dots in the response box from the other person, you wait to see what they write before responding. Practice taming your tongue as you do in taming the text.

Brian Tracy, self-development author, says: "Attentive listening to others lets them know that you love them and builds trust, the foundation of a loving relationship."

E: Empathize.

How would you feel in another person's situation? Why are they telling you a story with so much emotion attached to it? Consider how you would feel if you were telling them your personal story. Don't respond with advice before you have thought about how you would receive the same advice. Be responsive not reactive.

I remember during a coaching session when a client told me he had an argument with his partner who had an issue with him leaving a towel on the bed. (It's never about the towel on the bed, by the way.) He told me he was trying to see her side and while patiently waiting for his turn to talk, he had the presence of mind to check off each word in the LISTEN acrostic. When he got to E, he listened to what she was saying and her belief that he was not contributing enough to the housework.

Seizing the moment, he suggested they go out for dinner at a restaurant. Over the course of the meal, he asked how he could lighten her load, promising to be more mindful of helping out around the house. He immediately lifted his game and after two weeks of stepping up, he found the relationship improved dramatically.

We rarely spoke of his wife in our sessions after that, and if we did, it was in celebration of how happy they were together.

Author Krista Tippett hits the nail on the head: "Listening is about being present, not just about being quiet."

N: Never say "No" or "But."

Say, "Yes and ..." if you have a different opinion to someone else. Saying "No, no, no ..." discredits everything they've said, and "But, blah blah blah ..." will switch them off. Unfortunately, many people stop talking before they ever get a chance to be heard. It's worth considering what Steve Hawking said: "Quiet people have the loudest minds."

CONCLUSION

"In your actions don't procrastinate. In your conversations don't confuse. In your thoughts, don't wander. In your soul, don't be passive or aggressive. In your life, don't be all about business."
—Marcus Aurelius

One of the earliest pieces of conversation advice I was given was to avoid talking about religion, politics, money, and sex. Apparently, there are some people who have no other content or subject matter to offer.

I've found that asking people what they do for a living and how they manage their family and work life is always a good conversation starter.

Things can get uncomfortable when you ask a person where they went to school or how old they are, because these are two things they can't change.

You can change your job and you can change where you live, so these subjects are good ways to find common ground. Some people only ask you where you went to school so they can tell you where they went to school.

I have a friend who attended a very prestigious school, and he takes immense joy in referring to the school I attended as "Povvo High" ("povvo" being short for poverty). But he has earned the right to be so obnoxious because I happily respond even more obnoxiously to his humor. A battle of wits is how our friendship formed and continues to grow.

I have this comeback up my sleeve when I meet a man who wants to tell me all about the elite private school he went to.

"I went to Knox," I say, referring to one of Sydney's most expensive boys' private schools.

"Oh, Knox Grammar?" he will respond.

"No, the school of *hard knocks.*" It always draws a laugh and we are able to converse from there, because humor is also a great way to unlock our empathy.

The difference between confidence and arrogance is self-assuredness and self-doubt. Many arrogant people are self-doubting bullies.

Confident people have a self-assuredness that comes from living their best life and wishing the same for others. They treat people with respect because that is how they want to be treated.

Today, I am writing from a beach café and witnessing a woman blasting a waitress because she, the customer, has burned her lips on her hot coffee. The man sitting across the table from her is also copping a spray because he has told her to stop shouting at the waitress. He'd better not leave that towel on the bed when he gets home …

I have always noticed that arrogant people are rude to waitstaff, cab drivers, and people in the service industry who can't really return fire because they might lose their jobs.

The pandemic brought out the worst in some people because under lockdown they lacked self-awareness and self-control and felt they could be rude or offensive to staff.

While I say, "Treat people how you would treat yourself," I think it better to say, "Treat people the way you would like to be treated," because I see evidence of people treating themselves very badly, all the time.

I hope that shouty woman with the burned lips experiences some joy in her day because perhaps there is more to her outburst and she is projecting troubles I can't even imagine.

It just means I'll have to give an extra big smile and a bigger tip to the waitress when I pay my bill, to help right the wrong she experienced. Paying it backward if you will.

Not all heroes wear capes and not all bullies wear school uniforms.

"Be kind, for everyone you meet is fighting a hard battle."
—Socrates

EXERCISE

"Few things tend more to alienate friendship than a want of punctuality in our engagements. I have known the breach of a promise to dine or sup to break up more than one intimacy."
—William Hazlitt, 18th-century critic

My father had a lot of sayings which often confused me as a boy but as I have grown older make a lot more sense.

When I returned from an errand up the street, he would ask: "Did you see anyone you didn't know?"

As with any small town, there were not many people that we didn't know. To people we didn't know, it was customary and polite to say hello.

This required confidence, and as a teenager I wasn't equipped with much self-confidence.

Most strangers probably didn't hear my shy, inaudible greeting. But that didn't stop me saying hello, because it was easier to say hello than to be judged rude. I think shyness and insecurity are linked to what we perceive others think of us.

Most shy people don't realize their shyness can come across as being aloof, because people they don't know wonder why they would be shy, given all that they have going for them. I have known many attractive and talented people who think less of themselves and present in a way that hides their shyness under a veneer of rudeness.

Arthur Schopenhauer said: "Politeness is to human nature what warmth is to wax."

Another of my father's sayings was: "It wasn't that you forgot, it was that you thought so little of it, you didn't think it worthwhile remembering."

I offer this thought to you from a keeping-of-promises perspective. People will judge you as a person who lacks authenticity when you break engagements with them or show a lack of punctuality.

My good friend Ralph Anania, author of *Life Done Right*, says, "On time is late." Arriving late to an engagement shows that person or client that whatever else you were doing was more important.

I have a lot of fun giving keynote speeches and speaking to audiences around time management. I often ask for a show of hands from anyone who has ever been late to a job interview.

There are usually only a few who raise their hand, and they usually do it with a grin.

But when I ask: "Did you get the job?" their humor quickly subsides, and the rest of the room starts to laugh.

The English playwright E.V. Lucas sums it up perfectly: "I have noticed that the people who are late are often so much jollier than the people who have to wait for them."

So, how's this for a social experiment?

1. Think of combining your activities and join a friend for a walk. Spiritually, you're in the great outdoors, physically you're moving, financially it's still free, and mentally, as Nietzsche says: "All truly great thoughts are conceived while walking." Plus, you're socializing.

2. Where in your environment (and let's not discount that worldwide web) can you connect and engage with people with a simple "Hi, my name is … what's your name?"

3. Widen your social network: consider joining a book club, gym, or spiritual weekend retreat. Think about studying at night college, doing an online course or a course within a Facebook group.

4. Repair old relationships with family or spend more time with people who are important to you.

5. Ask a colleague something about themselves that you have always been curious about, or speak to someone in the workplace you've never previously said a word to.

6. Organize a regular date night with your partner or a close friend. Tell your family about your day and listen to them when they see an opportunity to share a common thread. Don't just listen to content, listen for context as well.

7. Where are you showing disrespect to friends, clients, colleagues, and family by forgetting engagements or being chronically late?

8. Seek out an octogenarian. People in their 80s have made lots of mistakes but have also learned lots of lessons. You give them the gift of your attention; they give you the gift of their wisdom.

Everyone has a story to tell. You will be amazed at how open people are if you show genuine interest.

I've had cab drivers tell me their whole life story on a 20-minute ride from the airport to the city, and the only words I've been able to get in are: "Wow, and then what happened?" and "Hey mate, you missed the turnoff!"

> *"It is well to remember that the entire population of the universe,*
> *with one trifling exception, is composed of others."*
> —John Andrew Holmes

6: Encouragement
The Daily Pursuit of Leadership

"Remember that when you leave this earth, you can take nothing that you have received—only what you have given: a full heart, enriched by honest service, love, sacrifice and courage."
—St. Francis of Assisi

INTRODUCTION

Saint Francis of Assisi is the patron saint of animals. A patron saint is someone who has been canonized a saint by the Pope.

Saint Francis of Assisi is said to have loved all animals and was even known to have preached to birds.

Saint Christopher is the patron saint of travelers. Many taxi drivers have a Saint Christopher pendant hanging from their rear vision mirror. Legend has it that Saint Christopher was about to cross a river when a young boy asked if he would carry him, too. Saint Christopher lifted the child on to his back and was surprised by how uncomfortably heavy he was for his size. Unbeknown to Saint Christopher, the child was the young Christ, carrying the weight of the entire world.

When Catholics pray for something specific, they can pray through a saint. I have found many a lost set of car keys after a Hail Mary to Saint Anthony, patron saint of lost items ...

Saint Jude probably has the toughest job on his hands, being the patron saint of impossible causes.

I like to quote Zig Ziglar when it comes to setting goals: "You are either a wandering generality or a meaningful specific."

So, for all the wanderers out there praying to Saint Christopher for safe travels, remember this aphorism: "God helps those who help themselves." Take the first step in your journey toward your goals and keep on going. And when you are planning your travels, pay for travel insurance.

Back to the saint who opened this chapter. One of my regular dad jokes is that Saint Francis of Assisi is the patron saint of email (A-ssi-si or "CC").

In cc'ing someone on an email, we are effectively including them. Inclusivity is one of the greatest forms of encouragement there is. We all feel compassion when we see reels, videos, or TikToks of a handicapped child being persuaded to have a swing and a miss to win the game of baseball.

Encouragement is verbal sunshine for the soul. In my youth, any teacher or adult who encouraged me got the absolute best out of me.

Dale Carnegie said:

"Tell a child, a husband, or an employee that he is stupid or dumb at a certain thing, that he has no gift for it, and that he is doing it all wrong, and you have destroyed almost every incentive to try to improve. But use the opposite technique; be liberal with encouragement ... let the other person know that you have faith in his ability to do it ... and he will practice until the dawn comes in at the window in order to excel."

I used to be friends with a woman who would often call her husband an idiot in public. I was so embarrassed by the way she humiliated him that I told her if she kept it up, that "idiot" would leave her.

Sure enough, he did. No one needs constant put-downs in their life.

As it has been said: "People have a way of becoming what you encourage them to be—not what you nag them to be."

This man wasn't nagged into idiocy, but he was encouraged into the arms of another woman.

On one memorable occasion I was encouraged not to be an idiot by the vice principal of my daughter's high school.

It was a fundraising event, and the vice principal's 30 years' service with the school was being honored. At our table, former students remembered her fondly. They told me she was as tough as nails but also encouraging.

During a break, I stepped outside with one of the other dads for a breath of fresh air. I spotted the vice principal standing alone in the corner of the courtyard having a cigarette.

I introduced myself and asked her what advice she would give to a father with two teenage daughters on the verge of adulthood.

She took a builder's drag on her cigarette and after exhaling like Clint Eastwood, looked me straight in the eye and said: "Never. Shut. The. Door."

"Oh wow, my daughters have both started keeping their doors closed all the time," I sighed.

"No, no, no, you idiot!" she yelled. "I mean, never shut the door on your daughters. Never shut them out, no matter what they do to disappoint you, or when they go against your wishes, because then you just deliver them into the hands of drug pushers, pimps, and any other miserable destiny you would never have wanted to wish upon them."

The German novelist Johann Wolfgang Von Goethe had something very poignant to say here: "Correction does much, but encouragement does more. Encouragement after censure is as the sun after a shower."

Why It Matters

I was chided by an elder one day, who said to me: "Do you think you might be giving your children a big head by telling them how great they are all the time?"

This was my response: "It will be easier to tell them to pull their heads in when they step out of line later in life because they will have been given the courage and confidence to change than it will be for me to tell them to grab the world by its borders after a lifetime of criticizing them or making them play small by not encouraging them."

When my firstborn daughter was seven, she would be put in "time-out" for seven minutes in her bedroom if she misbehaved. The rule was you spent one minute in time-out for every year you had been on the planet.

During one time-out, she wrote me a letter of discontent and slid it under her "cell door" to me. I responded with a poem and slid the letter back under her door: *"When you shout and when you pout, you must spend time in time-out."*

She responded in kind with a poem and the exchange went on for about fifteen minutes, rather than the seven minutes that her time-out should have really been.

I still have the written exchange, and I praised her at the time for her creativity, intelligence, and patience.

This was intentional. It encouraged her to repeat positive behaviors and discouraged her from poor behavior. As per the doctor's orders—"ignore what you reward and reward what you ignore"—I loved to praise my children and still do.

I read early on in my parenthood that you should praise your children so that they can hear you because they always hear our criticism but aren't around when we are boasting about them to our friends. This will encourage them to adopt and maintain the behavior you would like them to develop and repeat.

When I started school, I soon realized that my siblings and I were different from the other children and families. I arrived home one day with a permission note that would allow me to go on a school excursion to a place called Little Hartley Farm with the rest of my classmates.

I went to have it signed by my parents, but my three older brothers told me not to show my father and one said: "We're not allowed to go to school excursions. We've never gone to school excursions."

Believing I was special and different to my brothers, I ploughed on. After all, how could my father not let me go? But he didn't. And there was no explanation.

Throughout my childhood, "no" was often the answer, and my siblings and I didn't ask why, such was the fear and respect we had for our father.

I wasn't able to have playdates or go to birthday parties, nor was I afforded the luxury of new school stationery, new school uniforms, or football trading cards.

All the boys in my class and our school would collect and swap these cards with each other. It was a big deal.

One of my classmates was from a rich family. He had so many football cards it was ridiculous. Maybe close to 1000. One day, I asked my kindergarten teacher if I could be excused to go to the toilet. Seizing my opportunity, I grabbed 100 or so cards from his school bag, which was positioned outside with all the other bags, and quietly stuffed them into mine before returning to the classroom.

These cards were not like any I'd seen before. They were fresh from the packet and still scented with the bubble gum stick that came with them, unlike the scrappy cards my brothers brought home.

I can remember feeling a little guilty about what I had done, but mainly I was excited by the fact I finally had some football cards.

But moments later, a nun walked into the classroom and started whispering in my teacher's ear. We were all instructed to go outside in groups of three and retrieve our school bags.

I immediately sensed the jig was up. What could I do?

The older schoolboys would hang their sports bags on the hooks above the seats which covered our suitcases.

I waited for the other two students who accompanied me to return inside, and quickly popped my stolen bounty into a random sports bag.

The bag search revealed nothing, so once again we were sent back outside with our bags and once again I stayed a little longer so that I could retrieve the cards from one of the older boys' sports bag and place them back in mine.

I thought I'd gotten away with it. But it turned out there was a watcher on the wall, who had spotted me and she ratted me out to the nuns.

In front of the whole class, the nun bent me over her knee and shouted, "You sneaky little thief," smacking me four times on the backside as she emphasized each word.

I was then dragged by the collar and paraded in front of each class in the school in order to heighten my sense of shame. Adding to the embarrassment, nearly every class contained one of my siblings.

The final insult was that I was made to kneel for the whole day on cold floorboards and pray for God's forgiveness for breaking one of the Ten Commandments.

When my father found out that night, I was given a hiding, as you can imagine, and from that day forward I was known as "the sneaky little thief" in our family. If anything went missing at home, the first finger was always pointed at me.

Many years later, I returned to my hometown to attend a school reunion, and one of the first women I spoke with said: "David Lee, I thought you would have ended up in jail!"

I was taken aback. Why would she say such a thing?

"Well, you were the sneaky little thief," she added, "and you were always in fights in the playground."

Her friends laughed along with her and I felt that same sting of guilt and embarrassment again.

Mind you, I never ever hit anyone first, but I always stood up to schoolyard bullies and defended my siblings.

I have told this story to illustrate what the antithesis of encouragement is.

I might have been one of those who slipped through the cracks. I didn't have any malicious intention when I took those football trading cards. I am incredibly lucky I didn't believe or identify with the words of the nuns, the playground bullies, the teasers, and my siblings.

I could have worked on my "sneaky" and become better at thieving, to the point where I was a criminal doing time in prison just as my old school "friend" had expected.

Sadly, many people do identify with the negative labels that have adhered to them.

In my life coaching work, I help lots of clients remove limiting beliefs, which often manifest themselves from nasty nicknames or comments aimed at them by unthinking parents, siblings or "carers."

It's no surprise most people can recall that comment or criticism that started their decline in self-belief. Once that story is revisited and recognized as irrelevant to their current life purpose, confidence returns.

"Negging" is an act of emotional manipulation where a person makes a deliberate backhanded compliment or flirtatious remark to undermine another's confidence and increase their need for the manipulator's approval.

The term "gaslighting" comes from a 1938 play, *Gaslight*, which was made into a movie in 1944. In the film, the husband convinces his wife that she is losing her mind and her sense of reality so that he can have her put away into a mental institution and steal her inheritance.

Gaslighting and negging in adult relationships is possible because the "negger" or "gaslighter" has found a patsy, and when their victim reacts to the first bit of criticism levelled at them, they run with it.

In boardrooms, the antics of childhood bullies evolve into boardroom politics, which can have a devastating effect that leads to a pattern of acceptance and repetitive compliance.

I was fortunate enough to have an executive coach at a company where I was their top-performing salesperson. He told me his job was to rein me in and correct behaviors that my CEO at the time believed were ingrained and needed a "demons come out!" approach.

He said I needed to remove all emotion from my boardroom behavior. At the time, I would get upset and react when bosses bullied interns or were rude to people in the room. It also irked me when colleagues tried to undermine me by raising their eyebrows or sighing as I spoke.

The faces they pulled were designed to unravel me or create doubt in my mind, which used to work until I learned to believe in myself more.

The greatest improvements I made in my life at that time came from my executive coach's encouragement. He taught me not to take things personally and not to worry about the games people play.

He introduced to me the concept of "the toolbox fallacy," the idea that I thought I always needed more tools in my kit to be successful and accepted. Instead, he encouraged me to accept that I was more than enough as I was.

> *"It is easier to build strong children*
> *than to repair broken men."*
> —Frederick Douglass, American abolitionist

CHAPTER 26:

Serve Others

═══════

"The meaning of life is to find your gift.
The purpose of life is to give it away."
—Pablo Picasso

In their book *Ikigai: The Japanese Secret to a Long and Happy Life*, Hector García and Francesc Miralles write that there is no word in Japanese that means to retire in the sense of leaving the workforce for good.

The *Oxford Dictionary* defines *ikigai* as "a motivating force; something or someone that gives a person a sense of purpose or a reason for living."

In researching their book, García and Miralles spent time in the village of Ogimi on the Japanese island of Okinawa. Ogimi is known as the village of longevity. Its 3000 inhabitants enjoy the highest life expectancy in the world.

In Japanese culture, retiring and not keeping mind and body busy is considered bad for your health since it disconnects your soul from your *ikigai*. Being of service to the village by continuing to be involved in community life or continuing to work is felt to be a key ingredient to longevity.

In the book, 92-year-old resident Akira says: "Every day I wake up and go to the fields to grow tomatoes. Later I walk to the grocery store next to the beach and sell them. In the afternoon I go to the community center and prepare green tea for all my family and friends."

These Japanese people keep doing what they love and what they are good at even after they have left the office for the last time.

The French, of course, have a similar expression—*raison d'être*—which the Oxford Dictionary defines as "the most important reason for somebody's/something's existence."

The more time I spend with spritely elderly people, the more I find they are still involved in their community as volunteers or working the job they loved before they "retired."

Like a lot of the lessons much older people have taught me, we shouldn't wait until we're retired to adopt their youth-preserving behaviors.

The idea of using your skillset to be of service at schools and within your community can have a positive effect on your own happiness and well-being.

If you are a competent public speaker, volunteer to talk at high schools about your life's journey and the pitfalls you have experienced so that the next generation can benefit from your wisdom.

If you are technically minded, volunteer your services to help the elderly with setting up their Wi-Fi or other equipment in their homes.

When my children started school, I volunteered to cook at school barbecues, timekeep at athletics carnivals, and help with security at discos. I emceed school fundraising events, which were a blast because there was receptive audience with a shared goal, plus it was great practice for my own professional public speaking career.

Two of my sisters are teachers and one of them said at the time: "You will soon notice it is the same people who volunteer for everything, and other parents just leave it up to them all the time." I'm not sure if other parents were disinterested or disengaged, I just made sure I prioritized my involvement. I received so much joy and happiness from it that I figured "non-volunteers" just didn't get it, and deep down I was happy not to have competition for any of the roles.

As Mother Teresa said: "The fruit of love is service. The fruit of service is peace. And peace begins with a smile."

I was at an ATM near a busy train station withdrawing $100 and the machine dispensed two crisp $50 notes. As I turned around, there was a Salvation Army officer shaking a money tin for donations. I joked about my denominations being too big to depart with and he showed me that he had a tap and go machine which could accept as little as $10. So, I tapped and went.

As I was walking away, I started to think that for only $10 I felt as good as I would have felt after having had a one-hour massage. The gift of giving really is in the receiving.

I think this Zig Ziglar quote is important: "You can have everything in life you want if you will just help other people get what they want."

I think in helping other people get what they want in life, I'm well placed in my job to get what I want out of life. Happiness is all people really want to feel. That is the aim.

The definition of what makes people happy varies greatly, however. In his book *From Strength to Strength: Finding Success, Happiness, and Deep Purpose in the Second Half of Life*, Arthur C. Brooks believes that the three major ingredients to happiness are enjoyment, satisfaction, and purpose.

The satisfaction and enjoyment I receive from encouraging people to be better than they believe they are, and to press on in times of hardship, provides a real sense of meaning and purpose in my life.

I once had a client who was upset and anxious about the sale of her house because she had already purchased another one and needed the money to fund it. I felt a bit helpless because I didn't have a solution. She put her hand on my shoulder and said: "You have no idea how much you have helped me just by listening and encouraging me to trust in the process."

The Dalai Lama, when asked what surprised him most about humanity, replied:

> *"Man. Because he sacrifices his health in order to make money. Then he sacrifices money to recuperate his health. And then he is so anxious about the future that he does not enjoy the present; the result being that he does not live in the present or the future; he lives as if he is never going to die, and then dies having never really lived."*

I've coached many people who spent the first half of their life chasing wealth and are now spending the second half of their life chasing back their health.

Roses grow best with eight hours of direct sunlight every day. The idea of smelling the roses along the way seems to escape many people. Tend to the roses in your life with words of encouragement. Give them verbal sunshine every day.

"If you want happiness for an hour, take a nap. If you want happiness for a day, go fishing. If you want happiness for a year, inherit a fortune. If you want happiness for a lifetime, help somebody."
—Chinese proverb

CHAPTER 27:

Motivate and Inspire

"Parents learn a lot from their children about coping with life."
—Muriel Spark, Scottish novelist

O ne day I was talking to the seven-year-old daughter of my best friend and this is how the conversation went:

> Annalise: *"Do you know some people don't believe God is real?"*
> Me: *"Do you believe God is real?"*
> Annalise: *"Yes, when I talk to God about my problems, He answers me."*
> Me: *"What does he say?"*
> Annalise: *"Words of encouragement."*

Some might wonder where someone like self-help author Tony Robbins gets the energy to be as dynamic as he is, and how he still manages to have the energy to motivate and encourage himself along the way.

I was asked why after years of working in the dog-eat-dog corporate world I took the path of coaching. I'm no Tony Robbins, but my answer was that the most rewarding part of my job was never smashing sales targets or launching products and companies, but the cultivation of the people who achieved those goals either alongside me or under my tutelage.

A vested interest is where you have something to gain from the time you invest in a project or person. My personal stake in the development of my staff was that they would hit their budgets and we would share in the bounty of monthly and quarterly commissions and the celebrations that followed.

But more than that it was witnessing who those people became in the pursuit of their goals.

I was once phoned by a client asking for a favor. He had consumed a few drinks with his father-in-law and told him that he could get his son, who was returning from an extended overseas trip, a job interview.

He had to make good on his promise and asked me to at least have a coffee with his brother-in-law.

Coincidentally, I was hiring at the time for a sales role and my budget for an annual salary was around $80,000.

I met with the young fellow in a café, and even though it looked like he was wearing his dad's ill-fitting suit, he was a nice guy and we talked about his time overseas working in bars and surfing.

He only had a tiny bit of tele-sales and door-to-door experience, but what impressed me most about him was his enthusiasm. I discussed the role with him and asked what sort of money he was looking for.

He stammered: "$35,000, maybe $40,000?" He was very apprehensive.

I told him I'd start him on $40,000 but added that if he did everything I asked of him in the three-month probation period, I would double it to $80,000.

Some things were quite menial. He did all of my administrative work, but we also did lunchtime workouts, consumed Friday afternoon steaks and beers, and played games of pool, with me reminding him at every opportunity of the double salary promise.

I taught him everything I knew in sales, presentation, negotiation, and networking skills and allowed him to attend sales meetings with me. As he got more confident, he set meetings with clients himself.

Because he did all that was requested, after three months his base salary was doubled to $80,000 as I had promised.

At this time, I asked him to write out his top ten goals and show them to me. It was an important step, which I got him to repeat daily for the next month in the job.

After one year, he was earning more than double that $80,000 base.

We worked together for three years. One morning I called him into my office and asked him if he remembered writing his top ten goals for me after his first pay raise. I opened my top drawer and pulled out a sheet of paper which I had torn out of his notepad, with his top ten goals on it.

I read his goals out to him one by one. He had achieved nine of them, including buying his first home.

"There is one thing on this list that you have not yet achieved," I said. "Do you know what it is?"

He smiled. "Yes. It is to have your job."

"Well," I replied, "I resigned this morning and I have put you forward for my position.

He got the job and thrived in the role. He has since moved on and continued to kick goals in greater roles, winning industry awards and launching media companies.

As time has gone on, I have made a point of keeping in contact with former colleagues and mentees. Many have achieved phenomenal things. Some have risen to positions of power and leadership where they are now hiring and encouraging protégés in the same way I did with them.

In my opinion, they all succeeded because they were driven and responded well to praise and encouragement. I am yet to meet a person who doesn't.

When I recall their journeys and the small role I played in them, I feel absolutely fantastic.

"Caring about the happiness of others, we find our own."
—Plato

CHAPTER 28

Lead with Empathy

=====

"Would I rather be feared or loved? Um ... easy. Both! I want people to be afraid of how much they love me."
—Michael Scott, *The Office*

My management philosophy was the same as my life philosophy: right the wrongs without vengeance.

It's not the bite of the snake that kills you, it's chasing after that snake that sees the venom course through your veins. Venom is the hatred you carry inside, or the sadness you experience each time you recall that time someone wronged you.

My favorite revenge quote is from Jerry Seinfeld quoting George Herbert: "The best revenge is living well."

I raised my children the way I wish I had been raised. I coached my daughter's sports teams the way I wish I was coached, and I managed colleagues the way I wish I had been managed.

And that was with empathy and encouragement.

In his book *The 8th Habit: From Effectiveness to Greatness*, Stephen Covey defines leadership as "communicating to people their worth and potential so clearly that they come to see it in themselves."

As a staff manager, I didn't like the method known as the "praise sandwich." The idea was to deliver praise, followed by criticism and then praise again. I praised staff as they achieved, and again afterward to inspire them to greater success.

One of my bosses prided himself on the Machiavellian management theory: "It is better to be feared than loved because you can control fear." He would always say this when he was drunk.

My approach was the polar opposite. I asked employees how they felt after a particular presentation or sales call and where they felt they could do better next time then told them to do exactly that.

I coached my youngest daughter in soccer to three consecutive grand finals, two of which we won. We were no different from any other team, but we trained more nights a week than other sides and focused on the idea that a great team will always beat a team of great players.

One of the girls' mothers asked me after a particularly incredible comeback what I had said to the girls at halftime because they had played so poorly in the first half.

At halftime I always had the girls follow me to the middle of the field far from their parents. Why? Because I didn't want them to hear any more criticism from them. Some would be shouting at the girls from the sideline. Others would be calling their daughters out as lazy in front of their teammates.

When we got to the center of the ground, I would ask the girls where they thought they weren't performing, and they would sort out among themselves what was not working and what they should do about it. They literally coached and inspired each other. Before they started the second half, I would send them off with a motivational speech, with the idea these words of encouragement would stick with them in the moment and into the future.

I gain great encouragement myself from these same girls now that they are young adults whenever I see them in my local area. Working in local restaurants, they remind me of my words of encouragement from which they benefitted as I benefit from the bonus cocktails they send to my table.

Encouragement requires you to consider making the lives of the people you encounter better for having spent time with you. They will be wiser for having learned from you, and the example of humanity and humility you have demonstrated will linger in their memory.

"Humility is not thinking less of yourself," C. S. Lewis wrote, "it is thinking of yourself less."

When you have empathy for other people, you lighten the load of their worries and stresses. You may even find yourself having another Jerry Seinfeld moment. This time it will be: "I'm a good person."

But as I learned in my sales days, you can't sell a secret and you can't lead with empathy by keeping your compliments and positive feedback a secret and to yourself.

Holding them back in the belief that tough love is leadership is like holding your breath in the belief that you are conserving oxygen.

> *"It is not titles that honor men, but men that honor titles."*
> —Niccolò Machiavelli, Renaissance thinker

CHAPTER 29:

Be A Mentor

"You give but little when you give of your possessions. It is when you give of yourself that you truly give."
—Khalil Gibran, author of *The Prophet*

Apart from Machiavellian management styles, there is another huge problem I have witnessed and had recounted to me by many women in business.

It is not so much that they have had to overcome misogynists in the boardroom, but that they have had to overcome *miss-ogynists* in the staff room.

Countless women have told me most of the roadblocks they faced on their way up the corporate ladder came from other women spreading rumors about them or belittling them.

We've all heard the phrase the "glass ceiling." Much of the glass-ceiling commentary is around men creating a boy's club and not allowing women to ascend the corporate ladder, which I believe has been true throughout history.

The following definition is taken from *Frontiers in Psychology*:

"Glass ceiling refers to the fact that a qualified person wishing to advance within the hierarchy of his or her organization is stopped at a lower level due to a discrimination most often based on sexism or racism. The glass ceiling refers thus to vertical discrimination most frequently against women in companies. The difficulty inherent in this theme is the diversity of definitions and approaches describing the glass ceiling."

I was told a story many years ago by a very wise old man whose daughter was struggling with the glass-ceiling effect in her workplace. He explained to me that in the old days of live theater and traveling carnivals, there used to be flea circuses.

The performing fleas were trained in glass jars of varying heights. The fleas would jump and hit their heads on the lids, and after repeating this several times, would jump slightly lower so that they wouldn't hit their heads anymore. That meant that even when the lid was taken away, they never jumped higher than what the height of the lid had been and remained stuck in the jar.

The wise old man's point was that the glass ceiling was for some an imaginary obstacle that had created the limiting belief that women who believed in its existence would never make it to the top because they were encouraged to think it impossible.

Fleas can jump 220 times their own body length and 150 times their height. That's equivalent to a human being jumping over the Eifel Tower.

Fleas don't have wings and they don't jump that high because of powerful leg muscles. There is a pad of elastic protein called resilin above the hind legs of a flea that enables them to propel themselves like Superman.

Resilin and resilience are related words. They stem from the Latin verb *resilire*, meaning to rebound or recoil.

Resilience is your personal self-encouragement. It is the ability to bounce back from defeat and overcome adversity. Resilience is not looking for people or theories to blame your failures on. It is about taking personal responsibility.

It is possible to develop a "friendtor" relationship, where you mentor friends through shared experiences.

With the glass ceiling and *miss-ogyny* in mind, beware of the "frenemy," the opposite of a friendtor. They were once confidants and supposed friendtors but had really been jealous or envious saboteurs all along.

To be able to mentor a colleague is an honor. If someone wants you to be their mentor, you can decide whether the relationship is worth investing in by asking them to read a book you highly recommend.

If in a week's time they have not started reading it, they have shown they probably won't be very responsive to what you suggest, and you have saved yourself a lot of time.

One of my mentors was shocked that I had read a book he recommended in under one week. *The 48 Laws of Power* by Robert Greene is over 400 pages. My mentor had told me it was the solution to the problems I had with a tyrannical boss and a colleague who had slandered me in the workplace for monetary gain.

It's first two laws are as follows: Law 1: "Never outshine the master"; and Law 2: "Never put too much trust in friends."

The promise that this book held for my peace of mind made me want to read it. I wanted a solution to my problems. That is my nature. I want to solve a problem in the quickest way so that I can get back in control of my happiness.

The back cover of *The 48 Laws of Power* reads: "A book for those who want POWER, watch POWER, or want to arm themselves against POWER." After reading it, I realized I knew very little about power, which is probably why I couldn't put the book down.

The reciprocity of mentoring is such that your mentee can become a lifelong friend, facing life's challenges with you. I still catch up with my mentors at least twice a year and often get unexpected phone calls or text messages from mentees updating me on their successes.

Elanor Roosevelt said: "Great minds talk about ideas, average minds talk about events, and small minds talk about people."

I think from time to time, we might find ourselves in a situation where the conversation has moved through all three of Mrs. Roosevelt's scenarios. Be careful about who you choose as your mentor. Be aware of the responsibility that comes with mentorship and the confidentiality it entails.

Beware of those who have built their glass houses and live in small-mind town. Avoid this town and its gossips. They will bring you into their world and relay your story to any small-minded person who will listen.

Don't take the words of oppressors too harshly, and use their derogatory comments as reassurance that you are on the way to the top.

As Oscar Wilde said: "It's when people stop talking about you that you have to worry."

It has been the mentors in my life whom I have relied upon for wise counsel in dealing with tough times who have kept my trust and confidence and taught me resilience.

It is the gratitude I have for my mentors that has encouraged me to mentor others. I tell mentees they just need to turn the heat up on their burning desires, because even glass breaks at temperatures of 150C (302F).

It is the words of gratitude I have received from my mentees that fill me with joy and a peace of mind.

Once I learned I was a mentor in a 21st-birthday speech—much to my delight. The 21-year-old was the son of my first and greatest mentor outside of my family. (Yes, you can mentor siblings, children, and even parents, but remember the words of Jesus: "A prophet is never recognized in his own home.") I used to babysit this young man when he was a curious toddler asking me question after question, and regardless of my answer, always following up with "Why?" Funnily enough, the birthday present I gave him was *The 48 Laws of Power.*

> *"Let no corrupting talk come out of your mouths, but only such as is good for building up, as fits the occasion, that it may give grace to those who hear."*
> —Ephesians 4:16

CHAPTER 30:

Pay it Forward

═══════════

"The scent of the rose remains on the hand of the giver."
—William Shakespeare

My younger brother Brendan is a very wise priest. He often tells me that my one goal in life should be to get to heaven.

Father Brendan has told me there are ten commandments, and they are not known as the ten suggestions for a reason. He also talks of sins of commission and sins of omission. By that he means it's not only the wrong that we do, but also the right that we do not do.

I believe we owe it to others to pay it forward. That is, we repay a kindness we have received by passing it on to a stranger as well as repaying the person who has done us the favor. Encouraging others by sharing the talents we have been born with is another way of paying it forward.

It is also suggested that we pay it forward by paying for an additional coffee so that the next stranger in the queue gets a free coffee or we pay for the next person's shopping at the supermarket.

The double-up here is that you feel good and the stranger feels good. The more you do it, the more people witness these random acts of kindness, and the more likely they are to repeat what you have done.

Some men distort paying it forward when they buy a woman they don't know a drink in a nightclub then get upset when she says: "Keep your drink, just give me the money."

Karma in Hinduism and Buddhism suggests that the sum of a person's actions in this and previous lives decides our fate in future lives. The modern use of the word approximates the phrase "what goes around comes around."

I had a boss who referred to this philosophy in his native Arabic using the word *kismet*. It comes from the word *qisma*, which means portion or lot, as in "one's lot in life."

"Lot in life" is usually used to describe bad luck or a negative state we are resigned to accepting. For my brother Brendan, heaven or hell is how much you have made of the Ten Commandments and whether your moral scorecard is positive or not.

Personally, I believe that in the here and now you will either be experiencing heaven or hell, or something in between.

As the great English poet and intellectual John Milton wrote: "The mind is its own place, and in itself can make a heaven of hell, a hell of heaven."

Ancient Chinese philosopher Lao Tzu is great on this: "Watch your thoughts, they become your words; watch your words, they become your actions; watch your actions, they become your habits; watch your habits, they become your character; watch your character, it becomes your destiny."

I like to add: "Be watchful of your destiny, it becomes your legacy."

All of Lao Tzu's "watchfuls" are consistent. Thoughts, words, actions, habits, character, destiny. They are all a collective of the things you do daily.

The idea of waiting until you die for your legacy to be fulfilled or remembered (legacy is literally defined as the monies or properties you leave behind) seems to me to be a hollow victory. If there is nothing on the other side, then whether you leave a lot or a little will be exactly the same, because you will never see the fruits of your legacy.

What will you be remembered for? Your legacy will be enjoyed, lived, and honored while you are alive if you encourage others to thrive now and into the future.

Encouragement's great kickback is that it kicks you back into self-confidence and self-happiness.

Serena Williams' coach Patrick Mouratoglou told her during her Wimbledon comeback a while ago that she won 80 percent of the games she played when she charged to the net for her opponent's drop shots. In fact, he had noticed she wasn't doing that at all.

She queried the figure as she most certainly knew she was giving up on returning them.

Mouratoglou told her the stats didn't lie. From that moment on, armed with the stats, she went on to win 80 percent of the games where she chased drop shots down, and in due course, took the Wimbledon crown.

Many shop assistants in fashion outlets tell their customers how beautiful they look in the clothes they are about to sell them. Retail therapy is much cheaper than psychological therapy and involves much less "unpacking," other than unpacking the new dress or suit that looks just as fabulous as the shop assistant told you.

Even if the words of encouragement you use are not entirely true, they might suit for the here and now.

I have gifted mentees or staff under my leadership with sales pitches and even sales that they otherwise wouldn't have been credited with so that they would gain the confidence to achieve results and wins of their own.

For sentimental reasons, I kept a letter my daughter Madeline had written to her tooth fairy "Fairy Floss":

"Dear Fairy Floss, it has been a while since I wrote to you, but I just lost another tooth, we have a two-story house now, and my bedroom is at the top of the stairs. I am in third grade, and I am nine years old. I lost my tooth but please don't forget me."

I have heard children as young as five or six tell other children that there is no such thing as the tooth fairy. Obviously, someone older decided it would be best if this impressionable child had their belief shattered early on. I opened the first chapter of this book with the story of how my fifth-grade teacher called me an idiot for believing in Santa Claus when I was 10 and ruined my Christmas.

The "age of innocence" is very brief and children have the rest of their lives to be troubled by the complications of adulthood. Let them be children for as long as they can. Adults who crush their children's dreams or stifle their imagination steal this innocence and carefree life stage. Be childlike yourself for as long as you can.

In Matthew 18:3–5 of the Bible, Jesus says: "Truly I tell you, unless you change and become like little children, you will never enter the kingdom of heaven."

I take it as meaning heaven on earth.

If you don't practice a childlike curiosity, daydreaming and cloud gazing now and again, then reality bites.

Children are experts at living in the now. They don't readily remember yesterday, and they look forward to tomorrow, but they don't fret about it.

Further on in Matthew 18:6, Jesus says: "But whoever causes one of these little ones who believe in me to sin, it would be better for him to have a great millstone fastened around his neck and to be drowned in the depth of the sea."

The New Testament God of Jesus and the foundations of Christianity are love, forgiveness, and repentance.

The responsibility of adults is to ensure that the children in their care are encouraged on the right path, so that they inherit the experience of heaven on earth. Swearing in front of young children or exposing them to age-inappropriate literature or media robs them of their age of innocence.

Similarly, discouraging children from following their dreams—or anyone for that matter—is a form of robbing it forward, certainly not paying it forward.

Choose words of encouragement carefully and the words you use to pay it forward. Make sure they benefit the stranger in the café queue or those in your circle of concern.

"The tongue is very small and light, but it can take you to the greatest heights and it can put you in the lowest depths."
—Imam Al-Ghazali, Muslim philosopher

CONCLUSION

"When the student is ready the teacher appears."
—Pumbaa, *The Lion King 1½* (and the Buddha)

Not everyone is open to encouragement. Choose your audience wisely.

You can lead a horse to water, but you can't make it drink. The horse needs to recognize that it may not be thirsty now, but it will be at some point in the future.

You have to make them aware of that. You have to choose the right time to deliver your words.

My best friend told me the first aphorisms I ever ran by her were: "Ask for forgiveness, not permission," and: "Always know your audience."

Twice I have had to ask for forgiveness from people who felt my encouragement was untimely or unwanted. Fortunately, they told me that what I said was beneficial, but the timing was off.

You have to know your audience. You also need to know whether they prefer the matinee or evening showing and whether they like outdoor cinemas. Some people are only happy when it rains.

Your audience may not care for what you have to say but that doesn't mean they don't need it. If someone starts telling their tales of woe, I ask: "Is there anything I can help you with right now?" They either give me the opportunity to assist or they maintain everything is OK.

If it's the latter, I can just listen and hear them out. Quite often the best encouragement is enabling someone to vent. To let go of what they are holding onto inside.

"Never underestimate the healing power of your quiet presence. It can bring more comfort than even the most eloquent of words."
—Writing on the wall of a palliative care unit

145

EXERCISE

"Three billion people on the face of the earth go to bed hungry every night, but four billion people go to bed every night hungry for a simple word of encouragement and recognition."
—Cavett Robert, orator

Here's how you can incorporate encouragement into your everyday life:

1. If a book has made a positive difference to your life, encourage someone you care about to read it. I have made countless life-changing gains and returns from setbacks after reading a book that was recommended to me by a mentor.

2. Volunteer to speak at a community center or school on a topic you know a lot about, with the overall objective being to inspire your audience in their journey.

3. Pay it forward by sponsoring a child who lives in poverty. The words of encouragement you will write to this child on their birthday and at other milestone dates will have an enormous impact for both of you.

4. Offer to mentor someone you know in the areas you feel they are lacking.

5. Encourage a stranger. They may even have the same struggles you face, and you will both benefit from the interaction. Look for the gifts in people that they don't recognize in themselves and encourage them to pursue and explore them.

6. Acknowledge yourself along the way for what you do contribute. Acknowledgement is the highest form of self-encouragement.

7. Coach a sporting team. It could be a colleague's or your children's team. It is enormously rewarding helping people find and utilize the talents they were born with. It also helps you manage people better.

8. Be the change you want to see in the world through active service in your community and through being involved in making your world and the world of others a better place. Encourage through your example.

"People will never remember what you said,
they'll never remember what you did, but they'll always remember
how you made them feel."
—Maya Angelou, civil rights activist

7: ENTERTAINMENT
The Daily Pursuit of Frivolity

*"The two best physicians of them all—
Dr. Laughter and Dr. Sleep."*
—Gregory Dean Jr.

INTRODUCTION

"There's a time and a place for everything" is said when people are mucking about instead of knuckling down.

I had originally planned to call the seventh E of Equilibrium the E of Escapism rather than the E of Entertainment. But increasingly, I realized that many of the E's are escapist in nature.

Enlightenment provides escape through meditation and clarity of mind. Education provides escape from the insecurity of misinformation and lack of knowledge. Exercise provides escape from the worries of premature aging and impending illness. Engagement provides escape from the fear of isolation. Encouragement provides escape from questions about the meaning of life.

Entertainment is also escapist. I have been known to slip away from life's responsibilities to watch the first showing of a blockbuster movie, like the *Matrix* movies or the *James Bond* films starring Daniel Craig.

Turning my phone back on and facing daylight after two or three hours in a dark movie cinema means I haven't had to reply to missed calls or messages. Nor have I thought about who was trying to contact me while I was "driving" in a car chase in Bond's Aston Martin through the narrow streets of Rome.

Fortunately, no crises are waiting for me. But before I go off the grid for two or three hours, I make sure those who need to know, know where I am.

When asked what I do for a living, I have two answers. One is, "I help people get out of their own way." Entertainment is getting out of my own way for the period I choose.

My other answer is, "I help people go from great to phenomenal." There's a time for entertainment and there's a time for balancing your other leisure activities to ensure you become phenomenal.

Most people say leisure means "fun." How many of your eight hours of leisure time are dedicated to seeking fun?

"Isn't this fun? Isn't fun the best thing to have?
Don't you wish you were me? I know I do."
—Dudley Moore as Arthur Bach, *Arthur*

CHAPTER 31:

Mindlessness

"A man who dares to waste one hour of his life
has not discovered the value of life."
–Charles Darwin

How much time do you spend scrolling through TikTok or other forms of social media, mindlessly watching random videos?

I did this for two nights running when TikTok was introduced to me during a period of COVID lockdown. It threatened to eat into my eight hours of sleep, so I went to bed two hours later to compensate for the time I'd wasted watching it.

But the next day I was two hours behind on my morning routine.

I had the luxury of being able to get up later, because I didn't have to commute to work, but I missed out on the activities I would usually benefit from in those first two hours. Watching the sunrise, for one.

How many times have you lost an entire morning from a hangover that was born from two or more hours of what I call 'Tip Top'? Where you kept on topping up your tipple and drinking yourself mindless in the name of entertainment?

How many times have you spent 45 minutes flicking through Netflix deciding what to watch and then gone to bed having watched nothing? Or perhaps you finally settled on something that lasted two hours but killed nearly three hours in front of the idiot box.

Do you remember when the television used to be called that?

Is your smart phone dumbing you down?

If you were to analyze your daily and weekly activities in half-hour blocks and realize what you are really doing with your leisure time, you would be astounded by how much time you waste in pursuit of mindless activities that only move you further away from your stated goals.

Examine the activities you use to procrastinate. Ask yourself, "Is this the best use of my time right now?"

Does the third episode of *Friends* from 1997 have any importance to your well-being today? If the answer is yes, then watch it.

You should prioritize what you feed your mind.

Here's the thing. How you spend your leisure time determines whether it and life will become treasured time, or sadly, lost treasure.

Having a plan for spending your leisure time is as important as having a plan for spending your working hours, whether that be behind a desk, out in the field, or beside an operating table.

If you see entertainment as getting smashed with your friends for a few hours, there is nothing wrong with that if you don't compromise your sleep and responsibilities the following day.

It is generally in the throes of a bender that you overeat, overreach, and overreact. Responsible drinking is where you still can respond. Irresponsible drinking is where you don't have the ability to respond. Drunkenness, as the Stoic Seneca said, is voluntary insanity.

Who you spend your entertainment time with is also important. If you feel anxiety about catching up with someone, then rethink the value of your time spent with this person.

If I meet a new PT client for the first time and ask them if they have any physical injuries, they might answer that they have "a dodgy lower back, damaged rotator cuff, or broken bones."

We would then agree that it is best not to deadlift. We would agree to avoid heavy shoulder moves and we would attempt to strengthen their bones through targeted weightlifting.

If I were to say to a new client in a life coaching session: "Where are your emotional injuries?" and they were to reply: "I have a dodgy friend who uses me and owes me money, I have a damaged relationship with my ex who makes my life miserable, and I have a broken relationship with my children, which makes me feel sad," we would have to work out a strategy to repair them.

We would agree that they should not continue "carrying" the freeloading friend. We would agree that they should avoid spending time with the ex, and we would agree that they should prioritize time to strengthen the broken relationship with their children.

In the same way, avoid people who drain the life out of your entertainment time.

The idea of spending time in the pursuit of frivolity is that it should be beneficial to your overall well-being.

Whereas Charles Darwin may have said man dare not waste an hour of his life, I believe the time that you plan to waste can be a golden time. The "entertainment hour," as I like to call it.

"The time you enjoy wasting is not wasted time."
—Bertrand Russell

CHAPTER 32:

Laugh

"A day without laughter is a day wasted."
—Charlie Chaplin

Once upon a time there was a very wealthy man who had twin sons. Their mother had died in childbirth and the father raised them as best as he could.

As they were approaching their tenth birthdays, he wondered whether he was bringing them up in the right way.

The firstborn son, Larry, was the Pollyanna of optimists, believing that his mum was still alive and that she may have run off to the circus, where he hoped he might find her performing one day. As a result, he had an overzealous obsession with the circus.

The second-born twin, Barry, was an abject pessimist. His mother had died in childbirth shortly after he was born, and he blamed himself.

The father was becoming worried that his sons were either too optimistic or too pessimistic. He wanted each of them to experience the other way of looking at life so that they might become more balanced in the way they saw things.

He had an idea to remedy the situation for their tenth birthdays. He went to the local toy store and bought every single toy, game, or puzzle a 10-year-old boy would like.

The night before their birthdays, he took the boys into the city where they had a lovely dinner in a nice restaurant and stayed in a fancy hotel.

At home, the twins had separate bedrooms because their father was very conscious that they needed to create their own identities, so while they were away, he had one of the bedrooms filled with all the toys he had bought and the other filled knee-high with horse manure.

The next morning when they returned home, he sent the twins to their separate bedrooms.

He sent Larry the optimist into the room full of horse manure and Barry the pessimist into the room with all the toys. Then he sat down to read the morning newspaper. Within seconds, he heard sobbing and wailing coming from one of the bedrooms and shrieks of laughter from the other.

"Yes!" he shouted. "Finally, they're cured."

He walked toward Barry the pessimist's room and found his son sitting on the floor crying. The father was shocked. What could possibly be upsetting him? "One of the guns on the 100-toy-soldier set is bent," Barry sobbed.

In the background, he continued to hear shrieks of laughter coming from the room full of manure.

As he opened the bedroom door and horse manure surged across the carpet, he found his son Larry, the eternal optimist, in the middle of it, jumping up and down shouting, "Daddy! Daddy! Daddy! Have you got a shovel? With all this horse manure, there is bound to be a pony in here somewhere!"

"The difference between an optimist and a pessimist? An optimist laughs to forget, but a pessimist forgets to laugh."
—Tom Bodett, commentator

CHAPTER 33:

Watch a Comedy

<hr>

"We don't laugh because we are happy,
we are happy because we laugh."
—William James

My best friend likes to end each day watching comedies on Netflix. This is how she unwinds. She finds it distracts her from the worries of her day. It is her way of "changing the channel" and allows her a good night's sleep.

I don't listen to the news or read newspapers, which is curious, considering I once worked for Sydney's most popular news and talkback radio station, and both major metropolitan newspapers. I don't consume news from any platform by choice because I like to be in control of how I prime my mood and mindset.

I'm not against television. We rarely watched commercial TV when I was a kid and were monitored and censored when we did, but now I have subscriptions to a few streaming platforms and I mainly take in comedies, YouTube tutorials, and *The Matrix*.

I'm fortunate enough to have a cleaner who charges $30 an hour. I encourage all my clients to get one if they are spending their weekends cleaning their homes. It promotes better use of leisure time.

I will ask my clients to consider what their hourly rate is: what they get paid each week, divided by 38 (the number of hours they work).

If, for example the hourly rate is $50, that equates to $1900 a week and just under $100,000 a year at $98,800.

That may be a lot or a little depending on who you are and your expectations in life, but I know many people who earn this kind of money who spend their weekends cleaning their house and then complaining about it.

Oscar Wilde said: "People know the price of everything and the value of nothing."

I believe your leisure time should be calculated at time and a half. Time and a half is usually the rate applied to an employee's wages when they exceed 38 hours during a work week. Overtime, as it is called.

So even if you are on $20 an hour, which is less than the minimum wage in Australia, at time and a half, that's $30 an hour for your leisure time. What does your leisure time equate to?

So be conscious of all areas in your life where you might be undervaluing leisure time.

In any case, I suggest we all change the channel and focus on making ourselves happy.

Watch a comedy every night on television for only one hour for your daily dose of the body's best form of medicine.

Whenever I hear the *Seinfeld* lines "Is that Costanza over there?," "Not that there's anything wrong with that," and "No soup for you!" I immediately start laughing. That's the effect you want.

> *"The world is a tragedy to those who feel, but a comedy to those who think."*
> —Horace Walpole, 18th-century novelist

CHAPTER 34:

Enjoy the Silly

═══════════

"Mix a little foolishness with your serious plans.
It is lovely to be silly at the right moment."
–Quintus Horatius Flaccus

Many years ago, I was complaining about my lot in life to my boss and hinting at the fact I might hand in my resignation.

"I don't think anybody really takes me very seriously here," I said.

"Do you even take yourself seriously, David?" my boss replied.

He asked me what other managers across the company might think about me. I told him I didn't care.

"Do you know what your problem is? You should care!"

My boss continued to lecture me on how I should carry myself and how frivolous and immature I appeared from time to time. He kept repeating the word "silly" to the point where he sounded quite silly.

"David, I need you to start caring what other people think of you, or you will never be anything but a salesman at this company," he warned.

I was at an impressionable age, so I took his advice. But straight away, my sales started to suffer, along with my self-confidence. My self-confidence was quite a new coat to be wearing anyway, so it was a double blow.

My boss was new to the company, and he continued to pile the pressure on, so I finally jumped ship to join another publishing company. I didn't leave a bad job like most people; I left a bad boss.

A few weeks into my new job, my new boss took me aside on a Monday morning following company drinks the previous Friday night.

"Do you know what your problem is?" he started.

I already had the feeling he was going to tell me I was silly, immature, and didn't care what people thought of me. But he didn't.

"You worry too much about what people think of you," he said.

He said the good humor and sense of fun I displayed on Friday night was a much more natural and authentic version of myself than the over-serious one I had been pretending to be in sales conversations and around the office.

He thought potential clients would warm to the real me and encouraged me to be myself.

I took his advice and began to enjoy work more. After initial greetings, I started off my sales calls with the same question: "Have you got time for a joke?"

The client would then often tell me a joke of their own. I soon became the top performing salesperson, and in three years, I had earned enough money from commissions and exceeding sales targets to buy my first house.

Paraphrasing Confucius, "When you love what you do for work, you'll never work a day in your life."

If you can set aside moments within your leisure time for some silliness along the way, you'll find life a lot lighter and easier.

At night, once my children were old enough to read to themselves, just before lights out, we would play a game we made up called "Sale of the Daddio," based on the TV show *Sale of the Century*. It was a game of 20 questions, and the first child to shout out their name got to answer the question.

I accompanied my youngest daughter to a television studio many years later for a TV game show she had been chosen to compete in called *Kitchen Whiz*. She and her friend had to answer questions about food and cooking against the clock and two other girls.

Unlike "Sale of the Daddio," all the girls had buzzers, and when the first question was asked, my daughter pressed the buzzer and shouted, "Madeline!" scaring all on set, including the host, who dropped her question cards. But she did answer the question correctly. Our silliness had paid off.

"We must eschew anything trivial. We must embrace all that is frivolous ... Trivial things take up all your time and dull your senses, whereas frivolity is meaningful, profound, worth living and dying for ... If we devote our lives to frivolity, the world will be a far, far better place. Humanity will be better able to fulfill its primary goal, that of having a good time."
–Cynthia Heimel, sex and relationship columnist

CONCLUSION

"There are moments when one has to choose
between living one's own life, fully, entirely, completely, or
dragging out some false, shallow, degrading existence
that the world in its hypocrisy demands."
—Oscar Wilde

In his book *The Art of Making Memories*, Meik Wiking, CEO at The Happiness Research Institute in Copenhagen, suggests that memory is triggered by associations, tastes, smells, songs, and multisensory experiences.

Apparently, Andy Warhol changed his perfume every three months, for the sake of creating new memories.

I can think of no more multisensory experience than laughing. A sitcom is by definition a situational comedy. Look for situations where you will find yourself laughing. That might be in a comedy club, in the office kitchen, or even while smiling at yourself in the mirror for one minute priming your happy hormones.

A meaningful life is a life full of meaningful memories.

Dr. Suess said: "You never know the meaning of a moment until it becomes a memory."

"Groundhog Day" is an expression people use to convey how their life feels when it seems repetitive and boring. It comes, unsurprisingly, from the movie *Groundhog Day,* a 1993 American fantasy comedy film starring Bill Murray as Phil Connors, a cynical television weathercaster covering the annual Groundhog Day event in Punxsutawney, Pennsylvania.

He becomes trapped in a time loop, which forces him to relive 2 February over and over.

There's a similar theme, but with nastier daily consequences, in the 2014 sci-fi film *Edge of Tomorrow* starring Tom Cruise. Cruise's character dies every day in battle as he is sent to fight in a futuristic alien war. He also experiences a time loop conundrum, reliving each day, trying to find a way to defeat the alien invaders.

Bill Murray's character sees the monotony and his shortcomings and begins to make changes to his life. The other characters, unaware of his time loop predicament, are living each Groundhog Day for their first time, but in the course of the day they see the improvement in Murray's character and begin to admire him.

Tom Cruise's character remembers the dreadful things that caused his death and seeks out the training required to improve his skills so it doesn't happen again. Emily Blunt's seasoned soldier character trains Cruise, and each day he gets further and further through the battle until eventually he overcomes the aliens.

Once the credits stop rolling, I believe each day of our lives can be filled with little victories if we have a plan of attack.

It's easier said than done, but in the case of both Bill Murray and Tom Cruise's characters, they knew what each day would bring because they had seen it all before.

If you have the feeling that each day is every day or another yesterday, and you want to get the edge on tomorrow, write a plan!

"If you always do what you've always done, you'll always get what you've always got," McDonald's franchise founder Ray Krok wisely observed.

That is assuming nothing else changes. Nothing will change in your internal world if you don't affect it, but a lot can change in your external world which you can't affect.

Confucius said: "We have two lives, and the second begins when we realize we only have one."

Both Bill Murray's and Tom Cruise's characters worked at being better than they were yesterday.

Time flies, I hear people saying more than ever, regardless of their age.

The saying used to be "time flies when you're having fun," now it just seems to fly regardless. But you will remember the fun times when you have a plan for how to make the most of them.

Winnie the Pooh said: "You don't know you are making memories; you just know you are having fun."

My choice of social media is WeAre8, a social app where you control what you feed your mind, not an algorithm. You are encouraged to get off after only eight minutes, and with no anonymous users, WeAre8 promotes itself as a hate-free zone. It also pays you for watching advertisements. You can pocket this money or pay it forward by donating it to a charity.

If you are going to be on social media in your bedroom, stand up while you are at it and set an alarm to go to bed. It takes just as much discipline to go to bed early as it does to wake up early.

When your "go to bed" alarm goes off, leave your gym clothes out to save time and ensure that you train the next morning. Set up a Netflix comedy or YouTube session, ready to watch, when you turn your TV on, so that you have the time to be entertained and can laugh.

And to avoid entertainment time outweighing the other key areas of leisure time, set time limits on these as well.

Sleep stores key memories, so don't lose sleep over anything that isn't making you laugh. You are more likely to find things truly funny when you make the decision to look on the bright side of life and approach each day with the goal of maximizing the entertainment time available to you.

Everything is hard before it is easy. If you aren't setting the time aside to plan for fun throughout your day, then take the first step, even if it starts with telling yourself knock-knock jokes.

Rita: "This day was perfect. You couldn't have planned a day like this."
Phil: "Well, you can. It just takes an awful lot of work."
—Phil Connors and Rita Hanson in *Groundhog Day*

SUMMARY

"In the absence of clearly defined goals,
we become strangely loyal to performing daily trivia
until ultimately, we become enslaved by it."
—Robert Heinlein, science fiction author

Socrates said: "I am the wisest man alive, for I know one thing, and that is that I know nothing."

My parents chose the subjects I was to study throughout high school, so I clowned about during most of these subjects, particularly math. Math classes held zero interest for me. My mathematical education was pretty much limited to counting crows in the school playground after being sent outside for clowning about. In high school I even failed a math exam when we were allowed to use a calculator.

I remember with a laugh the words of old teachers telling me that I wouldn't be able to carry a calculator around with me all the time so I had better pay attention.

Me: "Hey, Siri! What's pi?"

Siri in her Irish accent: "OK, here's what I found. The number pi is a mathematical constant that is the ratio of a circle's circumference to its diameter, approximately equal to 3.14159."

I gave Siri an Irish accent because being of Irish descent, it instantly puts me in a good mood, and in my opinion, the Irish are the funniest and best-humored people on the planet.

Having performed poorly in the subjects my parents chose for me, I considered myself to be a poor student, until I found that I was able to focus on and retain information in subjects that I was interested in. Trivia is probably my best suit. A couple of years before I left home, I was given the board game *Trivial Pursuit* for Christmas. I lay in bed every evening memorizing the questions and answers and became very good at it.

A few years after I left home, on a return visit I took the game back with me to my city apartment.

A little while later, I had a small dinner party, and afterward I convinced my guests to play a game of *Trivial Pursuit*.

I had poured everyone a drink and was preparing to show off how smart I was using my inside knowledge of the deck.

But my anticipation soon turned to horror and embarrassment. We discovered that my parents had censored questions and answers they deemed too sexual or immoral in nature by drawing a line through them with a thick black marker.

Everyone else found it hilarious! Holding the censored cards under the light, revealing the thought control, they were particularly intrigued by what my parents deemed rude.

I remember one question from the sports category they had blacked out.

Q. "In horse racing, what is a gelding?"

A. "A castrated male horse having had its testicles removed."

It was the cue to come clean to my new friends about my strict upbringing, which they also found amusing. In fact, the laughter became so raucous that a neighbor called the police!

> *"Things which matter most must never be*
> *at the mercy of things which matter least."*
> —Goethe

EXERCISE

Consider planning the entertainment component of your leisure:

1. Limit social media scrolling and be conscious of how much time you waste. Download the WeAre8 social media app, reducing this time to eight minutes.
2. Smile at yourself in the mirror for at least one minute every single morning, until it's there before you've even recognized your face in that mirror.
3. Lighten up. Where are you taking yourself too seriously? Stop limiting the time you spend laughing by working so hard at being unhappy.
4. Look at how much overtime you are doing by spending leisure time doing household chores.
5. Seek out areas of entertainment where you can socialize and work at having fun. Go to more parties—better still, host one. (Get it catered if you can.) Smile at strangers.
6. Identify who your funny friends are and spend more time with them.
7. Program the comedy channel into your TV so that when you decide the time is right, you can slide into the couch for a guilt-free hour of fun and frivolity.
8. Think of a situation that is troubling you and ask yourself how you could make it funny.

"He who does not get fun and enjoyment out of every day …
needs to reorganize his life."
—George M. Adams, newspaper columnist

8: EMBODIMENT
The Daily Pursuit of Mastery

"Our deepest fear is not that we are inadequate. Our deepest fear is that we are powerful beyond measure. It is our light, not our darkness that most frightens us. We ask ourselves, 'Who am I to be brilliant, gorgeous, talented, fabulous?' Actually, who are you not to be? You are a child of God. Your playing small does not serve the world. There is nothing enlightened about shrinking so that other people won't feel insecure around you."
—Marianne Williamson, author and politician

INTRODUCTION

I have a theory based on thousands of coaching sessions, on human potential and endeavor:

I believe that only one percent of people *get it*.

By this, I mean that only one percent of people actually get what this life is all about and what needs to be done in order to live with purpose in the pursuit of happiness.

I believe you are one of this one percent.

But while 100 percent of the one percent *know* many of the secrets and steps involved in living the dream life, 99 percent of them *just don't do it*. It's no wonder Nike spent over 300 million US dollars on the slogan "Just Do It."

The difference between successful and unsuccessful people is that successful people don't want to do all the things they feel they have to do to be successful either, but they know that nothing will work if they don't, so they do them anyway.

In *The 7 Habits of Highly Effective People* by Stephen Covey, the greatest lesson I learned over and above any of the actual seven habits stemmed from this quote: "To learn and not to do is really not to learn. To know and not to do is really not to know."

When I quote Mr. Covey, I like to introduce one from Larry Riley: "True weakness in a person is recognizing that they have a weakness and not doing anything to correct it."

I had a client say to me once: "I know I need to do your program, I just know I don't have the time to do it right now."

My immediate answer was that once they had completed the written component, which is taking an inventory of their life, their subconscious gets to work on doing everything else they need in planning their destiny.

If you wait for every traffic light to turn green before heading into the city, it will never happen, and you will never start the journey. (Unless of course you need to put your makeup on, or you decide to eat a bowl of cereal with milk—then you never seem to get one single red light.)

All you need is willpower.

The will to DO what you know you must DO, the will to BE who you know you were born to BE, and the will to HAVE what you know you deserve to HAVE.

168

DO. BE. HAVE. DO BEHAVE!

I've been told to behave myself more times than I can remember, so I suppose it is quite ironic that I now tell my clients to behave.

When you DO what you say you are going to DO and you BE who you say you want to BE, you will HAVE what you say you want to HAVE.

Behavior is literally the way in which you conduct yourself. The repetition of how you conduct yourself makes a habit. As a veteran of the advertising industry and its methods, I know that in order for people to receive and act upon a message, they need repetition.

Repetition to the point that it becomes so annoying you complain to your friends about the advertisement and inadvertently promote it.

I took a huge risk in my early 30s, leaving the comfort a top job at one of the country's biggest newspaper publishers to join a start-up company in a sector of advertising I had never worked in—for a quarter of my "big wig" salary. The commission earning potential was huge. I was a new father, and my second daughter was on her way in three months' time.

In my new role I worked hard, and despite unreturned phone messages, ignored emails, and face-to-face knockbacks, I still achieved my annual sales targets within the first three months.

It was done through sheer persistence and patience. I had pinned to the wall in front of the telephone I used this quote from Calvin Coolidge, the 30th president of the United States:

> *"Nothing in the world can take the place of persistence. Talent will not; nothing is more common than unsuccessful men with talent. Genius will not; unrewarded genius is almost a proverb. Education will not; the world is full of educated derelicts. Persistence and determination alone are omnipotent. The slogan Press On! has solved and always will solve the problems of the human race."*

I received an award for my efforts. Inscribed on it was this Aristotle quote: "We are what we repeatedly do. Excellence, then, is not an act, but a habit."

And that is what embodiment is. The repetition of everything you know, the practice of all your powers, in action. The will to do, be, and have all that you were born to do, be, and have repeatedly with consistency until you do behave yourself into your ideal self.

Commitment gets you started, but you need to work on your goals consistently and with patience. Impatience is inconsistency.

Where there is a will there is also a way. And your willpower is your way. There is no mightpower, shouldpower, needpower, couldpower, wantpower, maypower or trypower in the dictionary. You will either use your powers or you won't.

"The only place where success comes before work
is in the dictionary."
–Vidal Sassoon

CHAPTER 35:

Willpower

═══════════

"There is surely nothing other than the single purpose of the present moment. A man's whole life is a succession of moment after moment. If one fully understands the present moment, there will be nothing else to do, and nothing else to pursue."
—Yamamoto Tsunetomo Hagakure, *The Book of the Samurai*

Most of the big or curious-sounding words I learned as a child I learned from my father. He didn't explain those words, and I very rarely questioned what they meant, because many of them were delivered during a stern disciplining.

He would often tell me to wake up to myself, but he would also tell me to use my *nous*. For quite some time I thought he was saying: "Use your *nows*."

In Greek philosophy, *nous* is the mind or the intellect.

Nous is most literally your common sense. The problem with common sense is that it is not all that common.

The 99 percent of the one percent of people who know what they should be doing with their lives right now but aren't, are not using their common sense.

The best way to use your *nous* is to use it now.

Willpower is directly linked to the power of now.

In the 18th-century poem "The Complaint: or Night-Thoughts on Life, Death, & Immortality," Edward Young writes:

> *Be wise today, 'tis madness to defer;*
> *Next day the fatal precedent will plead;*

171

Thus on, till wisdom is pushed out of life:
Procrastination is the thief of time,
Year after year it steals, till all are fled,
And to the mercies of a moment leaves
The vast concerns of an eternal scene.

Discipline is the next requirement alongside willpower and the now.

Discipline comes from *discipulus*, the Latin word for pupil or student, which is where the word "disciple" came from.

Early followers of Jesus Christ were known as disciples.

To be self-disciplined is to be a follower of yourself, but you need to know where you are going.

As Depeche Mode sang in 1989, you almost need to be a "Personal Jesus" to yourself.

No one cares or should care more about your goals than you. No one should ever tell you your goals either. People ask me what goals they should aim for, and I ask them: "What do you want and why do you want it?" The answers are your "whats" and your "whys."

The "whys" are the windows to your goals.

I don't like the motivational quote, "You came into this world alone and you will leave this world all alone" because it's not true and it is a distortion of the original words.

In most cases, we are born to a loving mother and loving parents, and how you live life determines how you leave life.

The actual quote originates from the Hindu text the Bhagavad Gita: "Always remember one thing. You came alone into this world crying. You will go alone out of this world crying. In between these two you come across many objects which are not belonged to you. There is no use in crying for these objects. Always try to be happy with yourself."

When you procrastinate, you lose sight of the big picture. There's been many a day throughout the course of writing this book that I almost convinced myself going for a walk was better for my thinking and creativity than getting through the "writer's block" I was experiencing. I had to stop and ask myself what my overall goal was. My procrastination mind would say, "Walking will give you peace of mind," but my rational mind would say, "Finishing this book will give you greater peace of mind."

On one afternoon of procrastination many years ago, I decided to visit a clairvoyant.

I had been told about this clairvoyant by a mother from my children's school, who raved about her uncanny accuracy. The psychic told her that her child was being bullied. The mother had not recognized symptoms of bullying in her child such as regular stomachache complaints and wanting to stay home from school.

One of my daughters had been complaining of an upset stomach and I was called by the school a couple of times to take her home. On each occasion, we would go to a café where I would continue to work on my laptop while she drank a chocolate milkshake with whipped cream—hardly the cure for an upset stomach.

When I visited the clairvoyant, I asked her about my children and whether they were being bullied. She pulled some cards out, asked for birth dates, and said: "You have a daughter who is being bullied at school and it's happening in a sporting environment, and she gets quite upset by this to the point of stomach pains." At this moment, I recognized that my daughter was in her sports uniform each time I collected her from sick bay.

She also told me that my other daughter was doing just fine. *Wow*, I thought. *Job done.*

"What about you?" she asked. "Would you like to ask me a question?" I politely declined and told her I was brought up a strict Catholic who wasn't supposed to consort with soothsayers. She laughed and told me that clairvoyants have been advising popes for centuries and that she herself was raised a Catholic.

"You've got 20 minutes left, why not get your money's worth?" she continued.

I relented. I told her my birth date and the year I was born as she requested. Then she said the number 8 was my "angel number" and asked me what sort of money I wanted to earn each year.

She flipped some more cards and told me to write the monetary number down. She asked me how far off I was from earning the money I wanted. She then told me that I'd had three past lives: one in Paris, one in Wales, and one in Egypt, and that in all three lives, I had been a writer.

I was a little skeptical, but I had been to both Paris and Wales and remembered feeling an affinity with them. I had yet to travel to Egypt, but I had a fascination for writing. She told me I was a communicator who would create programs incorporating acrostics and mnemonics, and I would write three books. I didn't know what an acrostic or a mnemonic was, but I'd always dreamed of writing at least one book—but hadn't started, of course.

Finishing up, the clairvoyant said: "Keep those notes somewhere you can see them often and read them regularly. Perhaps your underpants or sock drawer." (These were combined at the time.)

I returned home, and my daughter told me of a girl in her class who teased and mocked her sporting abilities. I met with the school principal and she gave my daughter a book that helped her deal with the bullying. The bullying stopped, along with the chocolate-and-whipped-cream milkshakes.

I did keep the notes in that drawer, and I did look at them regularly. I still have them to this day.

I have watched the sci-fi movie *The Matrix* more than any other because of the brilliant way it illustrates my theory that only one percent of people step away from the herd and get what life is really all about. In it, the main character Neo meets an intrinsic clairvoyant called the Oracle.

> Oracle: *"I'd ask you to sit down, but you're not going to anyway. And don't worry about the vase."*
> Neo: *"What vase?" [Neo knocks over a vase with his elbow. It falls down and breaks.]*
> Oracle: *"That vase."*
> Neo: *"I'm sorry."*
> Oracle: *"I said don't worry about it. I'll get one of my kids to fix it."*
> Neo: *"How did you know?"*
> Oracle: *"Oh, what's really going to bake your noodle later on is: Would you still have broken it if I hadn't said anything?"*

Of course, I did become a writer and I did create courses that rely heavily on acrostics. But what really "bakes my noodle" is whether I created those courses and earned the money she had said I would because of her predictions, or because I looked at what was written on those notes regularly and believed it was all achievable?

I believe the clairvoyant got me to write down goals that were greater than those I'd set myself previously, which were set within my self-perceived limitations.

My previous method of goal setting was more of a to-do list, rather than a plan for my dream life.

What the clairvoyant also got me to consider was the role our own actions play in our destiny and purpose, raising the age-old question of the meaning of life.

I arrived at the belief that life is about the meaning you place on the memories that you have and that you can create the memories you want to have, which will give your life more meaning.

I had started my sales training company by this stage, and I had already been working with acronyms I inherited from my earliest sales training instructors. I made the decision to work their old words into more meaningful words, which is how my programs developed into the use of acrostics and mnemonics; words that now meant something and were retainable.

I created words for structured sales training about why a salesperson would call a client and what problem of theirs the product would solve.

My sales training services accelerated into executive coaching.

I felt the first goal-setting acrostic I came up with (DREAM, outlined in the next chapter) had more meaning and impetus to it than the SMART goal-setting formula I had been taught, which was: Specific, Measurable, Achievable, Realistic, Timely.

> *"While wasting our time hesitating and*
> *procrastinating, life goes on."*
> —Seneca

CHAPTER 36

Be Accountable

"Comfort, that stealthy thing that enters the house a guest, and then becomes a host, then a master. And then it becomes a tamer, and with a hook and whip it makes puppets of your larger desires."
—Kahlil Gibran

The memories you have of events in your life are enhanced by the meaning these memories had for you at the time of their occurrence—happy, sad, or otherwise.

The more emotion that is attached to an event, the more vivid the memories. You recognize the value of what life means to you by the importance you place on a memorable event.

Identifying where you find your true meaning in life can help you identify your life's true purpose.

I like to ask people where they find their greatest happiness in life.

A simple two-fold question I ask is: "Where do you happily spend most of your time and money?"

Many men say: "Happy wife, happy life," and I always respond: "No, happy life, happy wife."

Some men meet a woman, display all the character traits she is attracted to, and form a solid relationship with her as a married couple.

Then an unfortunate life event happens. It's usually a loss of some kind. A job or someone close to the man, which makes him sad. His partner displays appropriate sympathy, and he takes solace in her support. But this behavior sticks as a newly adopted character trait for him. He becomes melancholic, which eventually becomes unattractive to his partner. She ultimately wants him to "man up" and be the person he was when he wooed her. Sympathy has become his new currency.

The perfect storm is when the man's melancholy coincides with the woman's menopause and the corresponding moods are bereft of kindness.

Postnatal depression is another instance where a partner needs to step up and be aware of the responsibility of "buffering the suffering" whenever they can.

These are all a crises of identity beliefs.

In the movie *Death at a Funeral,* a character says: "It's one thing to be in a bad mood, but a bad mood which lasts too long just becomes a bad personality."

Believing your happiness is dependent upon someone else is setting yourself up for trouble. It is putting your destiny in their hands. If you are a contented and unselfish person in the pursuit of happiness, the people around you should be glad that you are happy.

A lot of women I work with are dissatisfied with their husband or partner because he is unhappy and lacks vim and vigor. A lot of men I work with are dissatisfied with their wife or partner because she is unhappy and lacks vim and vigor.

To maintain a healthy relationship, both parties need enormous self-awareness and a sense of empathy, not sympathy. They also need a high level of personal accountability.

"You never really understand a person until you consider things from his point of view … until you climb into his skin and walk around in it," Atticus said to Scout in *To Kill a Mockingbird*, and I think he was right.

Many years ago, I realized I spent most of my free time in some form of fitness or health-based activity and a lot of my money was invested in the equipment and attire these activities required. I also spent time and money on buying and reading books. Mainly self-help books.

I have found great purpose and reward from personal training and life coaching. So, it has made complete sense to combine both passions into mind and body coaching.

I developed a program that centers around the completion of a templated manuscript that enables clients to discover their life's purpose.

Throughout the process the question that is continually raised is "Why?"

This completed manuscript, which must be reviewed daily, then becomes a blueprint for their dream life.

I ask my clients to consider their manuscript in a Pavlovian fashion.

Ivan Pavlov was a Russian physiologist best known for an experiment that involved ringing a bell to signal he was about to feed a dog. Eventually he would ring the bell without supplying food and the dog would salivate at the mere sound of the bell.

In your completed goal-getting template, PAVLOV stands for:

Portable: able to be easily accessed and taken with you to review.

Actionable: a list of realistic and actionable desires, not merely wishes.

Verifiable: you have proof as time goes on that you are closer to what you want to achieve.

Learnable: it is who you become in the pursuit of your goals.

Optimistic: you must believe positively in your goal's achievability.

Visible: not hidden away in a phone or laptop, or in your mind.

Just like Pavlov's dogs, the sight of this document should make you "salivate for your future." It holds a mirror to yourself and serves as a template for exploration and accountability. If the eyes are the windows to the soul, then the whys are the windows to your goals.

Here is a synopsis of the PURPOSE acrostic I created to outline the process:

Planning. Life management requires you to have a plan. Failure to plan is planning to fail. What are your daily routines and habits? Your routines are fundamental to your overall purpose. Within that overall purpose, plan morning and evening rituals.

Understanding your starting point. Rate yourself across what I call the "8 Masts of Mastery": Mental, Physical, Spiritual, Social, Financial, Family, Business, and Romance.

Reviewing the lessons you have learned in life and the setbacks you have had, and reframing the way you look at these from an empowering perspective with a plan for renewal. See the mistakes you've made as lessons, and then do everything in your power to ensure they don't happen again.

People. Who is on your team? Where are you involved in your community? Which people do you have to cut ties with who are hindering your growth?

Optimism. You must have a confident expectation that everything you set your mind on will become inevitable with the right set of plans. What would your dream life look like if you knew you could not fail and everything went to plan?

Solutions. What structures do you need to put in place? What is working for you and what is not? What problems will your plan solve? What is the worst thing that could possibly go wrong?

Effectiveness. What is the best use of your time right now and every day to ensure that your overall purpose is purposeful? What is the first step you need to take?

The reason I use acrostics as mnemonics is to ensure your objectives are memorable, retainable, and actionable. Your PURPOSE manuscript and blueprint needs to be read and reviewed daily, preferably right before journaling, because you should be living your life with PURPOSE.

When I started my coaching business, the mnemonic I created for attaining goals was based on encouraging people to write their goals with their DREAM life in mind.

The SMART goal acronym lacked motivation for getting people to take action to attain their DREAM life.

I created the DREAM acrostic model to help you list your goals to start living your dream. It is intended to be applied across every area of your life.

"If you dream it, you can do it," Walt Disney said.

Within the 8 Masts of Mastery, ask yourself what you desire to achieve:

Desire: What do you absolutely desire in your life from a mental, physical, spiritual, social, financial, family, business, and romance perspective?

Realistic: Is what you desire achievable?

End time: Dreams without deadlines remain dreams. When do you expect you will achieve your desires?

Action: What are the action steps you need to take in each of these areas?

Make it happen: Take the first step and then the next …

What can you do right now as you pen your dream life plan to make it a reality?

Only you know. Only you can make your dreams come true. Only you have that desire. Only you can put an end date on them.

Once you start to realize these crucial points, you'll take responsibility for your life. If you think it's someone else's fault, you're not living your dream and you've obviously given that person control of your life. Take it back! Author William Johnsen said something I've been repeating for years: "If it is to be it is up to me." I've since changed this to remove any doubt. I don't use the "if" word any longer. Quite simply, there are 10 two-letter words that will determine your future and they must become one of your daily mantras: "*As* it is to be, it is up to me." Once you identify what your "it" is and why "it" matters so much within each of the 8 Masts of Mastery, go after each "it" relentlessly.

> *"Do or do not, there is no try."*
> —Yoda

CHAPTER 37:

Self-belief

---

*"That's been one of my mantras—focus and simplicity. Simple can
be harder than complex: you have to work hard to get your thinking
clean to make it simple. But it's worth it in the end because once you
get there, you can move mountains."*
—Steve Jobs

When I first started working for myself as a sales trainer, one of my workshops involved public speaking and presentation skills and was called "Turning the Spotlight off Yourself."

Everybody sells. Selling is telling. I am now in the job of selling people on themselves, uncovering and telling them their features, advantages, and benefits. Selling is also about relationships. People buy people and then they buy their products. People buy products from people they know, like, and trust.

In order to sell someone on themselves, they need to get to know, like, and trust themselves and they do this by identifying their unique features, advantages, and benefits. *Fab*!

I encourage people to have mantras or affirmations that they write and read—ideally out loud—as a source of comfort and reassurance. They must always involve "I."

I am … I will … I have… I drive … I live…

Toolbox fallacy, as I said in the Encouragement section, prevents people from making their dreams come true because they think they're not quite ready enough to act on them. But you already have all the tools in your toolbox; more isn't always better. No one has the perfect preparation for their journey. So don't stall. Life rewards action!

I have an interstate friend who loved to show me his "vision board"—a standing whiteboard in his office with terrific ideas and dreams written all over it. But each time I visited, I noticed that his vision board was just that. He wasn't doing anything other than writing what he wanted out of life on the board. So, I asked if I could borrow his marker, crossed out the "VISION" header, and replaced it with "ACTION." As Bill Gates said: "Vision without action is daydreaming."

My friend went on to set up offices in three countries around the world and now has three beautiful children.

I asked an emergency surgeon how many people who present to emergency do so because of a life-threatening accident. She said the figure was around 75 percent. Of the remaining 25 percent, 20 percent would not have had to go to emergency if they led healthier lives. The remaining 5 percent presented as fit and healthy, but they thought they were having a heart attack. In reality, they were having a panic attack.

I have had high-performing executives tell me that in the pursuit of their dreams, they feel as though they might be having panic attacks. So, I asked my daughter Annabelle, who is in her final year of her master's degree in psychology, how anyone would know whether they were having a panic attack. And she said, "Well I guess you don't realize it is actually a panic attack until you don't die."

And you won't die if you go after your dreams, but you will die with enormous regret if you don't.

"Life is short, break the rules, forgive quickly, kiss slowly, love truly, laugh uncontrollably and never regret anything that made you smile. Twenty years from now you will be more disappointed by the things you didn't do than by the ones you did. So, throw off the bowlines. Sail away from the safe harbor. Catch the trade winds in your sails. Explore. DREAM. Discover."
—Mark Twain

CHAPTER 38:

Gratitude

———

"Gratitude is the memory of the heart."
—Jean Baptiste Massieu, 18th-century French bishop

I am incredibly grateful that the terrifying father of my youth became the most gentle, supportive, and loving man of my adulthood.

My father was nobody's fool. At 25, I met my uncle Eamon on a trip to Ireland. He told me that my father collected 14 of the 15 academic awards at his high school graduation in Galway. It was my trip to Ireland and the letters I wrote home to my parents at the time that seemed to right all the wrongs with my father and cement our relationship. He praised my writing and story-telling abilities in the letters he sent back, and he gave credit where credit was due from those days forward. From then on, we played many games of golf together and shared drinking sessions as only the Irish can do.

On one of those occasions, a person who had a little too much to drink asked: "How can you laugh and drink with this man after the way he treated you as a child?"

My father looked at me with an expression of sadness I'd never seen before.

I piped up. "I am who I am because of the restrictions and coercions of this man," I said. "I am very happy with who I have become, as opposed to who I may have become had this man not been dedicated to encouraging my education and formation. So, thanks, Dad. Cheers!"

At my father's 85th birthday party, he exhibited all the positive traits I ask my clients to imagine having when they reach that age.

My father was the epitome of the "muscularity 85-year-old" I write about in the E of Exercise section.

At the party, he stood up straight and strong, having risen from his chair unaided, and articulately thanked all his loved ones for attending. He was grateful for the loyal friends and family in attendance and spoke about his love and care for them. He of course singled out my mother for special praise and finished his speech by saying "You're all great," his voice trembling with emotion.

Early the next morning, as I was leaving to return to my home in the city, my father was in the kitchen, and I received my first ever bear hug from him. He felt so much gratitude to all his family.

My father passed away peacefully in his sleep without any warning exactly three months after that day. Two days before he died, he walked four kilometers to see his doctor and came home with the good news that his blood pressure was 120 over 80, which is considered excellent at any age.

I had watched a game of football with him and my brothers a couple of nights before and joked with him that as much as I felt I was in trouble a lot as a child, many of the really naughty things I did were so well planned that I got away with them.

The day after my father passed away, my sister Monika and I were upstairs in our family home looking through my father's belongings.

She said: "When they say in the Bible that it is easier for a camel to pass through the eye of a needle than it is for a rich man to enter the gates of heaven, that certainly applies to Dad, because he had no possessions of any value."

There were mainly books, photos, and golf paraphernalia that he had received as birthday, Father's Day, or Christmas presents from his children.

I remembered a song my father sang when I was younger from *Porgy and Bess* about having plenty of nothing, and that being plenty.

My father had been keeping daily journals since 1998, chronicling the events of each day. He recorded his exercise, phone calls received from family members who had visited him, and any other significant family events. He was quite often the family memory bank. He would say things like: "Do you know that it was 12 years ago today that you had that knee operation?"

Reading through his journals, it struck me how many times the word "great" appeared in them. It seemed he had cracked the code on what an attitude of gratitude and a purposeful existence is all about. An attitude of "greatitude"!

I read the eulogy for my father on the day of his funeral, referring to my sister's comment and his journals. I said that my father's greatest possessions were the wonderful memories contained within them.

His greatest possessions lay not in material things, but in his family. His family was his greatest possession.

To get to sleep of an evening, ask yourself what three things you are grateful for from the day you just had. Not gratitude for things like the weather or the trains running on time, but gratitude for the events, people, and connections you really appreciated. What truly great things formed the memories of your day?

When you think of what you have in life, what you lack disappears.

When you think of what you lack in life, what you have disappears.

I think the best sleeping tablet is a clear conscience. When you have given a good account of yourself for eight hours at your job, you will feel satisfied and productive.

If, during your eight hours of leisure time, you have worked toward berthing at the eight ports which the 8 E's of Equilibrium offer as safe harbors, being truly present in the now of each moment, you will experience balance.

You will also get a night of good restorative sleep where, with an attitude of gratitude, you will dream of "found treasure," knowing that you have collected meaningful memories from your day.

You will be sleeping on and creating what you will have embodied on that day: your memories and their meaning.

"Memories are the diary we all carry with us."
—Oscar Wilde

CHAPTER 39:

Perspective

═══════════

"If you are depressed you are living in the past. If you are anxious you are living in the future. If you are at peace, you are living in the present."
—Lao Tzu

In his book *Man's Search for Meaning*, which I believe should be mandatory reading in every secondary school, Viktor Frankl, an Austrian-born, Jewish psychiatrist, chronicles the time he spent during his incarceration in four Nazi concentration camps.

In 1944 at a camp hospital, he observed that the death rate was at its highest between Christmas Day and New Year's Day.

Frankl attributed the spike in deaths to the many prisoners naively holding out hope for liberation before Christmas. As the end of the year drew closer and it became clear that nothing would change, they lost courage and hope. This impacted their power of resistance and their desire to survive.

It was those prisoners who were able to retain their sense of personal identity that had the greatest peace of mind and highest rates of survival in the concentration camps. Frankl noted that survival and self-preservation depended more on mental and emotional strength than physical strength.

He established that healthy survivors had three key coping methods:

1. **Purpose**: Despair, Frankl posited, is suffering without meaning. Once meaning is established, tragedies can be turned into personal triumphs.
2. **Goals for the future**: Prisoners were stripped of their identities, possessions, and dignity, with no idea if or when their day of freedom would arrive. Those who still maintained belief in their goals and hope for the future were able to persevere.

3. **Rich inner lives**: Prisoners who had rich inner lives coped much better than those who did not. Something as simple as appreciating the beauty of a sparrow perching on the barbed wire fence surrounding the concentration camps became important. Religious or spiritual beliefs, prayer, writing—as Frankl did—vivid imaginations, love of life, and most importantly, a sense of humor (dark as it may have had to be at times) were also key.

Frankl writes: "Humor was another of the soul's weapons in the fight for self-preservation. It is well-known that humor, more than anything else in the human make-up, can afford an aloofness and an ability to rise above any situation, even if only for a few seconds."

He also placed great emphasis on attitude.

"Everything can be taken from a man but one thing: the last of the human freedoms—to choose one's attitude in any given set of circumstances, to choose one's own way."

Frankl's insights, borne out of surviving one of the worst atrocities in human history, have had a tremendous effect on me. Obviously, my childhood experiences can in no way be compared to the horror of the Holocaust, but thanks to Frankl, I now have an entirely different perspective on how I view my upbringing. Things could have been far, far worse.

When I was 10, I complained to my mother that I always felt I missed out on things in our family. As the middle child, I was either too old to do what the little kids were doing or too young to do what the big kids were doing.

I remember at a carnival watching as each of my siblings received money to play the laughing clowns or to try to extract a soft toy from the claw crane machine.

I was whining about the unfairness of it all to my mother. Basically, I was playing the martyr. A martyr sees what is happening and does nothing about it, looking for someone to blame and gaining a sense of ironic joy from disappointment.

My mother handed me a two-cent coin, pointed to a wishing well, and said: "OK, sad sack, why don't you throw this in the well and make a wish that you are in a different family?"

I took the coin and thought of taking her advice. I even thought of pocketing the coin. Instead, I closed my eyes and said to myself: "I wish that I wasn't so sad all the time, and that I could be happy all the time." Then I dropped the coin in the well.

My mother told me not to tell her what I wished for and held my hand warmly, which made me happy. *It's working already*, I thought. Later that day as we walked to the train station, every person I passed smiled at me. I began to think immediately that my wish had been granted.

As we found our seats on the train, my mother handed me two plastic-wrapped sandwiches, which I expected to be frozen as per usual. But they weren't. They weren't beetroot and ox tongue either! They were peanut butter, which was my favorite.

At the next stop, two hulking men sat down across from me, and I felt a little afraid as I ate. But one of them smiled at me and said: "Hungry, big fella?" We all broke into laughter. My wish was being answered at a rapid rate.

I soon developed an enthusiastic sense of optimism, and always found the ability to laugh regardless of the situation.

There is a profound quote from Friedrich Nietzsche that has inspired me to this day: "He who has a why to live for, can bear almost any how."

I had found my "why." To be happy all the time, so that I wouldn't be sad.

There was only one sure way to be happy all the time. That was to choose to be happy and to do the things I knew I needed to do, which would bring happiness about all the time.

An empowering spin on the Lao Tzu quote that opens this chapter is that if you are nostalgic you are living in the past positively, if you are optimistic you are living in the future positively, and choosing to be positive in the present is to be at peace right now.

The "now" is measured as three seconds. We can survive for three weeks without food, three days without water, and three minutes without oxygen. How long can we survive without being positively present and happy in the now?

I believe I was granted my wish to be happy all the time and have been ever since. And I have found that laughter is the best medicine for any unhappiness, so I have been overdosing on it for as long as I can remember.

"The attempt to develop a sense of humor and to see things in a humorous light is some kind of a trick learned while mastering the art of living. Yet it is possible to practice the art of living even in a concentration camp, although suffering is omnipresent."
–Viktor Frankl, *Man's Search for Meaning*

CONCLUSION

*"You have given me an infinity within the numbered days,
and for that I am eternally grateful."*
—John Green, *The Fault in Our Stars*

As I said before, we rarely watched commercial television as children, but we were allowed on occasion to watch movies as a family of a Saturday night. My parents censored the advertisements by turning the TV off for three minutes each time the program went to a commercial break.

Often the break didn't quite last three minutes so we would have to guess what had happened.

The first movie I remember watching as a child was *The Wizard of Oz* starring Judy Garland. It starts in black and white and changes to color once Dorothy, caught up in a tornado in her hometown in Kansas, ends up in the land of Oz, where she is greeted by the good witch Glinda and hundreds of munchkins who sing her the directions to her destiny via a yellow brick road.

Along the journey to the Emerald City, home to the Great Oz, provider of all that one desires, the main character Dorothy and her little dog Toto are joined by the Scarecrow; who wishes he had brains; the Tin Woodman, who longs for a heart; and finally, the Cowardly Lion, who seeks courage.

When they reach the Emerald City, they discover they each already possessed everything they believed they needed to achieve their happiness. They face many trials along the way, but they overcome them all, often because of the Scarecrow's good thinking, the Tin Woodman's compassion, and the bravery of the Cowardly Lion. They embody all that they are and reach their destiny.

This movie stuck with me for a few reasons—the least favorable being the scary-looking winged monkeys who wreak havoc on the four travelers …

More importantly, it struck a chord because each character had doubts about their own capabilities yet continued their quest to achieve happiness.

As the Scarecrow found, brains are not the same as an intelligent and developed mind. It's what goes into those brains that becomes an adult's mind. Comprising 2 percent of a person's body weight, the brain is the most voracious consumer of our calorie intake, using 20 percent of the body's available energy. Some people can burn up to 500 calories a day just thinking. Some people burn far, far less.

As the Tin Man discovered, a heart doesn't necessarily mean you are a loving person. Random acts of kindness and altruism are actions of a loving person. People treat you the way you encourage them to treat you. I have found that a person incapable of giving love is also incapable of receiving love. Which were they incapable of first? The giving or the receiving? I'm pretty sure when they first believed they were unlovable, they decided to pull back on offering love. While the scent of the rose remains on the hand of the giver, as Shakespeare said, the rose remains in the hand of the giver if the recipient won't accept it.

The Cowardly Lion believes he lacks courage and is a coward because he experiences fear when lions are supposed to be the kings of beasts. He believes that his fear renders him inadequate. He does not understand that courage is acting in the face of fear. Courage requires you to trust yourself and trust the process. The Cowardly Lion is in fact brave, but he doubts himself.

Confidence breeds courage. Most arrogant people are insecure chest-beaters—bullies of sorts—who when faced with real danger, back down and fall to pieces. The Cowardly Lion jumps out from behind a bush to scare Dorothy and her new best friends, only to scare himself in the process when she smacks him on the nose.

Confident people have a preparedness about them, and courage borne of the fact they have done their homework and are ready for the worst. "We sweat in training to avoid bleeding in battle," armed forces recruits are told.

The Wizard of Oz pops into my mind when I meet people who forget or are completely unaware that they have everything they need inside of them right now to reach their DESTINY (which I'll expound on in the next exercise). They have either forgotten who they are or believe that who they once were is gone and lost forever. And they lack a plan.

I recommend that you take the plan for your DESTINY one day at a time, one lesson at a time, one step at a time, one meal at a time, one meeting at a time, one connection at a time, one social event at a time, one family event at a time, one romantic engagement at a time … with the acknowledgement that your planned DESTINY is inevitable.

EXERCISE

When people ask me why I am such a happy person I often reply: "Because I know how the story ends." (I don't tell them my wishing-well secret.) Of course, I don't know *when* the story ends. None of us do, but I'm confident that by doing what I do every day for my longevity and health span, it should end happily, recalcitrant buses aside. I am, however, intent on not wasting a moment of this precious gift called life. I practice what I preach and preach what I practice.

I love this inspiring quote from Oliver Wendell Holmes, a 19th-century essayist and humorist: "Many people die with their music still in them. Too often it is because they are always getting ready to live. Before they know it, time runs out." Our days are finite. None of us get out of this life alive.

This exchange in my favorite movie, *The Matrix*, also inspires me:

Morpheus: "Do you believe in fate, Neo?"
Neo: "No."
Morpheus: "Why not?"
Neo: "Because I don't like the idea that I'm not in control of my life."

It is with my destiny (not fate) in mind, knowing that I am doing what I need to do every day to get to where I plan to be at the end of my life, that brings me reassurance and happiness.

Here's the thing. How you spend your leisure time determines if it becomes treasured time, measured time, or tethered time. Start controlling how you live your life by writing out a "perfect day in the life of me" plan.

How would your perfect day look and feel? Break it down into choices and how you plan to respond to everything that comes your way, not to react. With a plan you avoid overwhelm. Rather than feel like you are spinning plates and when one falls, they all come crashing down, decide to have your plans as "irons in the fire": whenever one feels like it is dying down, stoke that fire with intentional effort.

At the beginning of each year, or right now even, write a letter to yourself starting with "It is (whatever the date one year from today is) and I have …"

I've been doing this for years. I remember reading my letter to my daughters on a beach backing off the holiday house we had rented in Hawaii. I said: "Hey girls, listen to this. It is 31 December 2018, and we are sitting on a beach in Hawaii, drinking French champagne, having just spent Christmas in New York after visiting Disneyland in California on the way through."

My daughters were bemused. "Look at the date," I said. "I wrote this on 2 January of this year, almost a year to the day."

I didn't just write it on 2 January 2018 and put it in a drawer. I read that letter every morning and every evening of every day and felt the feeling of that sandy beach, the queues of Disneyland, and the crisp winter air of New York City. I had followed the plan I set out for myself and never wavered from it. My friends call me DL. My very good friends call me DLTMM. David Lee The Magic Man! But there's no magic involved. Just discipline and hard work.

Like putting an undercoat of primer on a piece of outdoor furniture so that the top coat sticks and lasts, I prime myself every day to make sure I have a wonderful day.

The first thing I do every morning is have a cold shower for three minutes while a feel-good song is blasting in the background, a song which I have thoughtfully chosen the night before. The brand of soap I wash with is the same as we used in the shower of the holiday house we stayed in just twice as children and still reminds me of those good times.

The aftershave I wear has fond memories of the person who gave it to me. My deodorant recalls a European vacation more than 30 years ago, the sunscreen I apply reminds me of summer holidays all year round, and my morning alarm, "Forever Young" by Youth Group, reminds me to bring a fresh attitude to everything I do. I sign off my journal by writing, "I believe something wonderful will happen for me today," and I go looking for that wonderful from that moment.

Jim Kwik, American brain coach and author of *Limitless*, says: "Between B and D there is C. Between Birth and Death, there is Choice."

Choose your wake-up time, choose how much you drink of any liquid, choose to slow down your breathing, choose to take rest breaks, choose your daily movement, choose what you eat, choose who you socialize with, choose what you read, choose what you watch, choose how you think, and choose to think big! Most of all, choose life!

I hear of people complaining about the cost of living and I think, *What is the cost of not living?*

Consider how you will embody all that you have planned for your DESTINY and look at how you will incorporate each of the 8 E's into your day.

Keep your life's goal in mind by living out the DESTINY acrostic:

Do it now! Everything you want to be or have is on the other side of doing. As much as I say I'm always happy because I know how the story ends, no one is guaranteed the knowledge of when that day is, so there is no time to waste. Take a minute to begin it!

Energy and enthusiasm are the forces that enable you to achieve your life's goals. Never lose heart.

Success is inevitable. There is no way you will fail if you have planned a goal that is realistic and deadline-based with clearly outlined steps.

Trust the process. Trust is defined as the firm belief in the reliability, truth, ability, or strength of someone. With your beliefs and behaviors firmly established and a step-by-step process outlined, the only thing required is patient expectation and acceptance.

I am enough." You have everything you need within you right now and you know it.

Never ever quit. Not every day is sunshine and rainbows, but persistence is your brolly and shades.

You've got this! Yeehaw!

"Let us prepare our minds as if we'd come to the very end of life. Let us postpone nothing. Let us balance life's books each day … The one who puts the finishing touches on their life each day is never short of time."
—Seneca

LIFE CHALLENGE

"Challenges are what make life interesting and overcoming them is what makes life meaningful."
—Joshua J. Marine

So how do you pull it all together? How do you achieve the elusive work-life balance that the naysayers (pessimists) scoff at and the advocates (optimists) believe is in that room with the pony?

By starting with a morning routine and an evening ritual.

My morning routine is the rudder for my day. My evening ritual ensures I am anchored in for the night. The one is the antithesis of the other. My morning routine rudders are coffee, sunlight, and cold showers, and my evening anchors are chamomile tea, dimmed lights, and hot showers.

Plan your daily "SAIDYOUWILL" (schedule).

Do what you say you will do, as my daughter wrote in the opening page of one of my journals. Work out a schedule. Stick to it and prioritize your to-do list.

DO BEHAVE! What do you need to DO to be who you want to BE and have what you want to HAVE?

Your to-do list must become your "ta-da" list. Believe in magic and believe you are the magician.

As Napoleon Hill, the author of *Think and Grow Rich*, said: "Whatever the mind can conceive and believe, it can achieve."

"Work hard, play hard" was the mantra of the late 1980s when I joined the workforce. This was the era of long lunches and long workouts to balance all the excess. As a Libra, my life has always been about equilibrium. So, I changed this mantra early on in my career to "work smart, play smart."

Many of my clients feel their lives are out of whack right now. Whenever I told someone I was writing a book around work-life balance, that person would tell me it was needed now more than ever.

"Eight hours for work, eight hours for sleep, and eight hours for what we will" was the workers' battle cry during the Industrial Revolution. Workers subsequently achieved the 48-hour week through various on-the-job sit-downs and strikes.

The Ford Motor Company progressed the idea in 1914 when it scaled back from a 48-hour week to 40 hours after founder Henry Ford acknowledged that too many hours were bad for workers' productivity. In fact, I often repeat his maxim "If you think you can or you think you can't, you're right" when I'm talking about positive thinking.

Here in Australia, it was in 1927 that the Australian Conciliation and Arbitration Commission (ACAC) decided to reduce ordinary weekly working hours from 48 to 44. The 40-hour working week was adopted in 1947, and in 1983, the ACAC introduced the 38-hour week.

Some of my clients are working as many as 70 hours per week. Most work from 8:00 a.m. to 6:00 p.m. A far cry from the 1980 Dolly Parton song "9 to 5," 8:00 a.m. to 6:00 p.m. is 10 hours a week more than the ACAC legislated.

Think about this. Working an additional two hours a day per week, 10 hours times 48 weeks translates to 480 hours a year that you're taking away from yourself or your family and 60 extra workdays you are giving to your employer for nothing (assuming you take a four-week holiday).

The average weekly earnings for full-time workers in 2021 was $1713 (or $89,122 per year), according to the latest figures from the Australian Bureau of Statistics. That's $45 per hour.

If you multiply the 10 additional hours per week ($450) you are working by 48, that's a bonus $21,600 a year you are giving to your employer.

Every worker should adopt this anthem: "Eight hours of work, eight hours of rest, and eight hours to do with as I please; I'll turn my leisure time into treasure time with David Lee's 8 E's."

By adopting the simple framework of The 8 E's of Equilibrium, which are designed to be practiced sequentially and revisited throughout the day, you will create a more balanced and fulfilling experience.

If you can spend an hour a day on each of the 8 E's, you will find true value in your leisure time. You will find more commitment to your purpose. If you limit television and social media to one hour a day, you'll find you are more switched on and gain momentum much faster.

I have been encouraging clients to adopt the 8 E's of Equilibrium to make sure they are balancing the time they spend outside of work and sleep.

Eight hours' sleep is nonnegotiable. Any parent of a newborn or toddler knows why sleep deprivation has been used as torture in warfare.

We spend a third of our lives sleeping—determined by the fact that eight hours is a third of one day. If the average age at which we die in Australia is 85, this equates to over 28 years spent recovering and recharging throughout our lives.

If you trade sleep time for working late hours or binge-watching TV programs, you will suffer a sleep deficit that depletes your energy levels, and over time, erodes your general health and memory.

So, make sure you work all the time you are at work. You will have no reason to feel guilty or compelled to do unpaid overtime if you work honestly during your day.

"You don't have to make yourself miserable to be successful ... success isn't about working hard; it's about working smart."
—Andrew Wilkinson

THE EIGHT E'S OF EQUILIBRIUM IN SUMMARY

1. Enlightenment. Meditation, journaling, prayer.
"Knowing others is wisdom, knowing yourself is enlightenment." —**Lao Tzu**

2. Education. Learning and teaching.
"Education is the most powerful weapon you can use to change the world."
—**Nelson Mandela**

3. Exercise. Core/abdominal, LISS, MISS, HIIT, and healing.
"To enjoy the glow of good health, you must exercise." —**Gene Tunney**

4. Eating. Food as fuel.
"Bad men live that they may eat and drink, whereas good men eat and drink that they may live." —**Socrates**

5. Engagement. Connecting with your partner, children, the lonely.
"If you engage people on a vital, important level, they will respond." —**Edward Bond**

6. Encouragement. Verbal sunshine.
"Nine-tenths of education is encouragement." —**Anatole France**

7. Entertainment. Escaping the grind without being dumbed down by your "smart" TV or phone.
"Before machines, the only form of entertainment people really had was relationships." —**Douglas Coupland**

8. Embodiment. Practicing DO BEHAVE.
What DO you have to DO? To BE who you want to BE? To HAVE what you want to HAVE?

AFTERWORD

Throughout this book, I have quoted Larry Riley 10 or so times. Larry Riley is the pseudonym I use for myself because I am "as happy as *Larry* and I'm living the life of *Riley*."

I have my phone number in my list of contacts saved under the name of Larry Riley and have often sent myself text messages to excuse myself from a situation I feel is not the best use of my time.

It's a good hack for the devil's hour as well (3:00 a.m.) when I haven't paused at 3:00 p.m. earlier that day to consider what might keep me awake at that hour. These days, if I wake at 3:00 am, I say: "Hey Siri, send Larry Riley a text."

Siri asks what I want to say, and without having to do anything other than tell Siri what message to send to myself, the thought that disturbed my sleep is in my text messages when I wake up in the morning.

This moniker is designed to serve me like the mnemonics I employ as a constant reminder of what my overarching purpose is. I have a kinetic analogue wristwatch, which I wear as another reminder. If I wear it every day, I never need to wind it up. If I don't wear it for a couple of days, it stops and needs resetting, rewinding, and a couple of shakes to get it going again. Much like me, if I don't train daily. Use it or lose it.

I also carry a medallion in my pocket which has the words "*memento mori*" on one side, which means "remember you must die," and "You could leave life right now" on the other. There is also an image of a skull, tulip, and an hourglass. Mortality, presence, and time.

I believe we can use our leisure to just survive or to absolutely thrive. We laugh in the morning to avoid crying ourselves to sleep of an evening, and both ends of the day require us to develop a routine, so that our days aren't routine. The less conscious thinking you need to do, the more you can rely on your subconscious to work for you.

Time is your greatest commodity. Someone can rob you blind and if you are insured, you will see your possessions again. Even if you are not insured, you can rebuild your wealth and return to the life you enjoyed before. But theft of time is the greatest crime because you can never get time back.

Bruce Lee said: "If you love life, you will love time, for time is what life is made up of," and his life was cut short in his prime at the age of 32.

I once had someone yell out during a keynote presentation: "Why would you bother? What if you got hit by a bus tomorrow?"

I answered: "Well, at least I would fit in my coffin." These days I'm of the opinion that if I am consciously living my life by the standards required to reach 100 in good health, then even if tomorrow's bus caught me off guard today, up until that moment I would have been supremely confident, self-assured, and happy.

Planning all the way to the end also requires you to consider your legacy. Whether you leave a billion dollars or nothing, it will be of no consequence to you once you're gone. What is more important is that you live your legacy while you are alive.

As the great American spiritual teacher Ram Dass said: "You have all the time in the world, but don't waste a moment."

Live as an influential leader, with this LEGACY mnemonic to help you to remember to be remembered while you are alive:

Longevity. Sunshine, water, fasting, exercise, rest, and abstemiousness all contribute to a longer stay on this planet and enable you to enjoy the people you love.

Enthusiasm. Choose life. Be involved. Be a meaningful specific. Get at it and get after it.

Generosity. Give of your time. Be of service. Learn in order to teach. Be kind. Be so generous and giving that people don't want you to leave this earth.

Altruism. Be a philanthropist. Most billionaires realize that no matter how hard they worked, they can't stop working. The billionaires who start foundations have found a greater joy in what they contribute than in what they consume. You don't have to be a billionaire to experience this feeling. Volunteer your time and donate your money.

Consistency. Stay at it and stay after it. Employ any motivation you want. Inspiration is like showering. You must be inspired daily. My number plate starts with DDQ—David Doesn't Quit.

Youthfulness. "Forever young" should be your mindset. Some people die when they are 40 but we bury them when they are 70.

In his final year, my father gave me a lecture on the brevity of life after I had told him about a major life-changing decision I was about to make. He told me he had taken the garbage bins out for collection yesterday and seemingly again today, and that life seemed to go by faster as he got older. It's a truism for all of us.

One of his sayings was "we're not getting any younger, your mother and I," and I always thought he was joking because he would be standing strong and tall as he was delivering these words. But even if we appear as fit as fiddles and take every care to look after ourselves, life can be taken away from us at any time. *Memento mori*—remember that you will die. That is why we must be diligent about living our best life in the present.

We've all heard of the Latin phrase *carpe diem*, which means seize the day. The trouble with this phrase is that it gives you all day to do it when you really should be doing it now. I urge you to live by the lesser-known Latin phrase *carpe punctum*, which means seize the moment, because this moment is all that you have guaranteed. Do what you say you want to do right now. Then the moments will build into momentum for a momentous life.

I have a briefcase with a combination lock on it that contains all my precious memorabilia. It is filled with birthday cards, Father's Day cards, sporting ribbons, photographs, letters to and from the tooth fairies (Sparkles was Annabelle's tooth fairy and Fairy Floss was Madeline's), and other mementoes.

The words my father wrote on my 21st birthday card were: "We hope you have the success in life that we would wish you to have. God gave you all the abilities to achieve this end."

You too were born with all the abilities to achieve your end. Your job is to decide what that end will be and start pursuing it. Beginning now.

THE BEGINNING
Be well.
DL

"God has entrusted me with myself. No man is free who is not master of himself. A man should so live that his happiness shall depend as little as possible on external things. The world turns aside to let any man pass who knows where he is going."
—Epictetus, Greek Stoic philosopher

ACKNOWLEDGMENTS

I dedicated this book to my father, and I must acknowledge him for his tenacity in forging me into the man I am today. My mother, who doesn't feature as much as she should in this book, is a very private woman and having raised 10 kids, created the storyteller in me with the many stories she told me as a child. I am grateful for her encouragement along the way through her love and support to believe in myself as a writer.

Of course, I praise my two beautiful daughters Annabelle and Madeline, who have inspired me since the day they were born and make me so very proud to be their dad. They've heard most of this book throughout our walks and can finally stop asking me when it will be published.

This book wouldn't be possible without the editing skills of Ashley Gray, who was also the associate editor at *Australian Men's Fitness* magazine where we worked together and played many games of handball and darts, a work-life balance hack we practiced often.

I am very grateful to Shelagh Lubbock, who proofread both the first and second iterations of this book, the first of which was 50,000 words lengthier than today's.

I am very grateful to David Hancock of Morgan James Publishing New York for believing in this book's necessity and inspiring me to its completion, along with Naomi Chellis, Shannon Peters, and Jim Howard.

I am very grateful to the many clients whose sessions, achievements, and conversations formed the thoughts and ideas of this book and who have become great friends.

I would like to thank Dr. Celia Bentley for her foreword and for being living proof that the formulas contained in this book work despite the hours an emergency surgeon keeps.

Special thanks to Nicole Hazzard, who paid for draft copies of the original manuscript and encouraged me through her own personal success.

Leanne Blanckenberg from BMW, who inspired the writing of the 8 E's after hiring me as a keynote speaker three years running on Australia's national RUOK Day, which promotes positive mental health.

Alex Ranieri, founder of High Performance Fathers, who invited me to present and speak to his international tribe of men every second Sunday for the past three years, which challenged my way of thinking around men, women, and family and forged three of the E's, as originally there were only five.

To the friendtors: Tony Wren, Fergus Taylor, Hana Ayoub, Gareth Thomas, Ralph Anania, Cameron McClement, James and Carla Scognamiglio, Ben and Milly Marshall, Eric and Maria Pollard, Pete Jenkins, Ben Greenish, Tim Fernandes, Simon Percival, and Nickie Scriven. You have all inspired me along the way with your support and by challenging and growing my thinking.

I must thank my siblings, who have all contributed to the formation of my stories. My brother Kevin of course, my first and greatest mentor of all time, and special thanks to my brother Anthony for his mathematical calculations, my sister Monika for her constant encouragement and praise, my brother Terry for his constant check-ins, and my brother Brendan for the recall of many of our childhood memories.

This book was attempted six years ago yet sat on an old laptop. After rebooting the laptop during the pandemic and sending the original musings to self-publishing guide Emily Gower, who provided a manuscript template and told me I was on to something, I completed the first iteration in less than four months.

I would like to acknowledge and thank both Chelsea Greenwood and Arlyn Lawrence from Inspira Literary Solutions for the final typesetting and proofing and for their kind feedback on the inspiring nature of this book, which has given me the confidence to know that I have delivered my absolute best work for you, my inspired friend.

To my beautiful partner Batoul, who allowed me the space to write this book and who could quite honestly have the title of this book rightfully changed to *Conversations with David*. I am eternally grateful. You are an inspirational woman and have proven that while work-life balance is tough, it is not impossible. After many of these conversations and sharing her personal experiences, Batoul came up with the main title for the book, *Is Your Boss Making You Sick?*

Finally, to all the bosses I have had, and there have been many … The lessons I have learned from the good and the bad have taught me that no boss can ever make anyone sick, despite how much they might try. It is the ability to respond rather than to react to the pressures of work and to ensure a life outside of work from which you can establish identity and meaning that have made me as happy as Larry and allowed me to live the life of Riley.

ABOUT THE AUTHOR

David **Lee** is the CEO and co-founder of Leeway Mind and Body Mastery, an executive and leadership coaching agency specializing in work-life balance coaching programs that combine the elements of mind, body, and life to create harmony for any day and every day.

David is a qualified life coach, NLP expert, mental health practitioner, and personal trainer living in Manly on Sydney's Northern Beaches of Australia. David has worked high-pressure jobs for over 30 years and has also been a mind and body coach for more than 20 of these years. David was the in-house personal trainer for *Australian Men's Fitness* magazine for six years, which allowed him to test every imaginable fitness regime, diet, and nutritional supplement while meeting with some of the world's most exciting and accomplished sporting professionals and business leaders—including two prime ministers. David's ability to maintain peace of mind and keep his head while everyone around is losing theirs comes from a lifetime of studying the daily habits of philosophers, leaders, and CEOs, and through the daily curiosity he has had in human potential since his own childhood.

David found his greatest fulfillment in the corporate world through mentoring and coaching teams for personal and business success, which prompted a career shift: since 2002, he has been assisting both individuals and businesses in achieving their highest performance. David's programs employ "power" words and acrostics, which are mnemonics to ensure memorable and actionable content. He specializes in guiding clients toward peace of mind and physical empowerment, with a focus on setting and achieving goals through his unique DREAM goal-setting model. His workshops and one-on-one mastery programs teach participants the art of harmonizing mind and body for happiness, aligning with their life's purpose, creating daily habits leading to desired destinies, and the ability to live one's legacy rather than leave it behind. David is an accomplished keynote speaker and the creator of the work-life balance blueprint "The 8 E's of Equilibrium."

He has been a feature speaker for the past three years for "High Performance Father," a global company which has worked with over 12,000 men, and he co-authored the book *The Complete Health Series* in 2010.

www.mindandbodymastery.com.au

A free ebook edition is available with the purchase of this book.

To claim your free ebook edition:

1. Visit MorganJamesBOGO.com
2. Sign your name CLEARLY in the space
3. Complete the form and submit a photo of the entire copyright page
4. You or your friend can download the ebook to your preferred device

Morgan James
BOGO™

A **FREE** ebook edition is available for you or a friend with the purchase of this print book.

CLEARLY SIGN YOUR NAME ABOVE

Instructions to claim your free ebook edition:
1. Visit MorganJamesBOGO.com
2. Sign your name CLEARLY in the space above
3. Complete the form and submit a photo of this entire page
4. You or your friend can download the ebook to your preferred device

Print & Digital Together Forever.

Snap a photo

Free ebook

Read anywhere